George Sullivan

In the Wake of Battle

THE CIVIL WAR IMAGES OF MATHEW BRADY

Prestel
Munich · Berlin · London · New York

Contents

Introduction

The Civil War never goes away. The war's drama and violence and its status as a watershed event in American history lead scholars to keep studying the conflict and the general public to be continually absorbed by it. Many millions buy books, magazines, and videos, watch television documentaries about the war, and visit battlefields. Experts representing Civil War Roundtables probe fresh aspects of the conflict and tens of thousands shoulder rifles and dress in uniforms of the Blue or Gray to participate in reenactments.

The appetite for Civil War information leads inevitably to the photographs. No source is more authentic; few are as vivid and enlightening.

It's been estimated that a million or so photographs were taken between 1860 and 1865. And no wonder. There were 3,154 photographers active in the United States in 1860, writes Frederic E. Ray in *The Photographic Coverage of the Civil War.* "Almost every middle class family owned an album," notes Ray, "filled with portraits of their own, but also with copies of mass produced images of presidents, public figures, even actors and actresses." The *carte de visite*, a stiff rectangle of cardboard about the size of an ordinary playing card upon which a sepia-toned photograph had been mounted, was all the rage. Tens of thousands were sold.

Just as popular was the stereograph, a card bearing a pair of photographic images mounted side by side. When looked at through a stereoscope, a stereo card offered what appeared to be a three-dimensional image.

The booming market for *cartes de visite* and stereographs helped to expand the nation's roster of photographers. Mathew Brady, the photographer whose name is most closely associated with Civil War images, was well aware of the opportunity for financial reward that the conflict presented. Well before the first shots were fired, Brady, already extremely successful as a portrait photographer, had made up his mind to cover the war. It was not just for profit. He said that he felt a duty to do so. In photographing many hundreds of the most notable and distinguished men and women of the time in the years before the war, Brady felt he was acting as the nation's historian. He had the same feeling toward his coverage of the Civil War. He believed that he would be contributing toward building a record of the war's events.

Whatever his motivation, Brady is important because he organized and financed a corps of photographers and assigned them to areas of conflict. (While Brady sometimes accompanied his cameramen on their assignments, his poor eyesight prevented him from working as a field photographer himself.) Brady, who was said to have been present at the war's first battle, continued in his role as a coordinator of field photography until the very end of the conflict.

Several other photographers gained renown during the war. Scotsman Alexander Gardner (1821–1882) went to work for Brady in 1856 after immigrating to the United States, and was employed by him when he recorded a series of stunning scenes at the Antietam field of battle. After he split with Brady in 1862 or 1863, Gardner, with his brother James, opened his own studio in Washington, D.C., and went on to produce some of the Civil War's most memorable images. Many of these he included in his two-volume: *Gardner's Photographic Sketch Book of the Civil War*, published in 1866 (and available in a reprint edition). Shortly after the war, Gardner photographed those accused and convicted of conspiring in the assassination of Abraham Lincoln.

Timothy O'Sullivan (1840–1882) and James F. Gibson (b. 1828) are, like Gardner, frequently named as being among the very best of the war's field photographers. Like Gardner, they sharpened their skills as Brady employees before deciding to work independently.

With his photographs of Port Royal Sound, South Carolina, in November 1861, O'Sullivan was the first to document a Civil War battle scene. He continued to cover important battles and campaigns through the siege of Petersburg and the fall of Richmond, making a vital contribution to Civil War photography. Almost half of the photographs in Gardner's *Photographic Sketch Book of the Civil War* were taken by O'Sullivan.

James F. Gibson was, like Gardner, a Scotsman. He photographed with Gardner at Antietam, documented much of General George McClellan's Peninsular Campaign, the battle of Savage's Station, professor Thaddeus Lowe's ascension in his reconnaissance balloon, and even the famous ironclad Monitor. After the war, Gardner managed Brady's Washington gallery for a time.

George Barnard (1819–1902) became active as a photographer in the early 1840s, operating a daguerreotype studio, writing articles, and forming photographic associations. During the war, Barnard was an official photographer with the Department of Engineers and when General William T. Sherman's army marched from Tennessee through Georgia to the sea, then north into the Carolinas, Barnard traveled with them, photographing landmarks and battle sites.

His coverage resulted in his *Photographic Views of Sherman's Campaign*, published in 1866 (and available as a reprint). Barnard was later employed by George Eastman to help introduce the dry-plate process to the photographic community.

Andrew Russell (1830–1902), with training as an artist, learned photography in New York City. After he enlisted in the army in 1862, he became an official army photographer and was assigned to document bridge building, railroad construction, and other engineering enterprises. Russell also produced striking photographs at Marye's Heights during the battle of Fredericksburg as well as quality studies of Richmond in the war's final days. After the war, Russell became the official photographer for the Union Pacific Rail Way.

The Anthony brothers, Edward and Henry T., also played a key role in Civil War photography. From their offices and workshops at 501 Broadway in New York City, the Anthonys, using negatives made by Brady and other photographers, produced thousands upon thousands of small card photographs and stereographs to meet the public's demand.

The Anthonys functioned not only as publishers. They also were the nation's foremost provider of photographic equipment and supplies, offering everything from cameras and tripods, to picture frames and plate holders, to the great array of chemicals that photography required in those days—iodides and bromides, chloride of gold, acetate of soda, and double sulphate of iron and ammonia.

As this rundown suggests, Civil War picture making took much more than a camera and film. It was hard work that required special skills.

At the time of the war, photographers relied on wet-collodion-on-glass negatives that had come into wide use in the mid-1850s. To make a photographic plate, the photographer, working in a darkroom lit by red or orange light, poured collodion onto a perfectly clean and dust-free glass plate. When the collodion had set, the plate was bathed in a solution of silver nitrate to sensitize it.

After the bath, which lasted about three minutes, the plate was placed in a holder and then inserted in the camera, which had been set in position and brought into focus by an assistant or second photographer. Since the plate would stay wet for only about ten minutes, that was the amount of time the photographer had to make the exposure (which could last from five seconds to a full minute) and get the plate back to the darkroom to be developed, fixed, washed in water, and dried, and then given a protective coat of varnish.

For work in the field, Brady provided his cameramen with movable darkrooms which were built into the type of horse-drawn wagon that was widely used as an ambulance. Since an abundant supply of water was needed for photo making, each wagon was equipped with two 55-gallon water barrels.

In the years following the Civil War, many of the pictures taken by Gardner, O'Sullivan, Gibson, and other photographers were often attributed to Mathew Brady. This was no accident. This was because Brady normally designated photographs that were taken by his cameramen as "Brady photographs." This was a common practice among gallery owners at the time. But Brady did more. In his zeal to serve as the war's pictorial historian, he also copied prints made by other war photographers or acquired their negatives. Brady thus became a kind of archivist, eventually accumulating a massive collection of war photographs. Each was known as a "Brady."

After the war, Brady lacked the money to catalog and properly care for his acquisitions and they suffered greatly as a result. While the federal government eventually acquired the bulk of what Brady accumulated, many thousands of his photographs were scattered far and wide.

Today, the George Eastman House in Rochester, New York, lists 120 institutions that own collections of Brady photographs. What are termed "major" collections are in the hands of the Library of Congress, the National Archives, and the State Library in Hartford, Connecticut. "Substantial" collections are owned by thirteen institutions, including the Boston Public Library, Princeton University, and the George Eastman House itself.

Mathew Brady's financial problems contributed to the wide dispersal of his photographs. Before the Civil War began, Brady entered into an arrangement with the Anthony Company to mass produce and sell *cartes de visite* and stereographs from his negatives, with Brady receiving a portion of the proceeds.

At the same time, Brady was ordering huge amounts of photographic supplies from the Anthony brothers. The thousands of negatives that Brady placed in the hands of the Anthonys came to serve as security, as a guarantee that Brady would make payment for the items had been receiving. But Brady, struggling financially, was unable to square accounts with the Anthony firm. He had no choice but to relinquish the negatives, some 7,000 in number. They eventually ended up in storage in New York City.

The Library of Congress purchased these negatives in 1943. By that time, they had changed hands six times. Often they had been treated in a careless manner, suffering damage as a result. Some owners even added to the collection. On several occasions, the photographs had been used to illustrate Civil War histories, including Francis Trevelyan Miller's *The Photographic History of the Civil War*, a rather monumental ten-volume work published by the *Review of Reviews* in New York City in 1911–12.

The collection consisted of 7,500 original wet collodian glass plates, plus 2,500 copy negatives on both glass and film. These produced about 3,750 different views and 2,650 different portraits.

Once in the hands of the Library of Congress, Hirst D. Milhollen, a Library of Congress specialist in photography, and historian Donald H. Mugridge copied a selection of the collection's glass negatives that could be used in filling the public's order for prints. This project resulted in the production of 1,047 copy negatives, which were published on microfilm. They were listed and briefly described in *Civil War Photographs, 1861–1865: A Catalog of Copy Negatives Made from Originals Selected from the Mathew B. Brady Collection in the Prints and Photographs Division of the Library of Congress.* The catalog was published in 1961.

In making their selection, Milhollen and Mugridge endeavored "to include the best and most interesting photographs." Left uncopied were scenes that varied only in a minor detail from those selected as well as views that were particular favorites of Brady cameramen and often repeated. Pontoon bridges and companies of engineers are two views in that category. Negatives that showed deterioration were rejected, although some of the more dramatic views were printed from cracked glass plates (and appear in this book).

The Brady Collection at the Library of Congress is only part of the story. Besides the collection of negatives that ended up in the hands of the Anthonys, Brady had a second set of some 6,000 negatives which he placed in storage in Washington, D.C. In 1874, these negatives were sold at auction to the U.S. government for $2,840, the amount required to satisfy an unpaid storage bill. The following year, Congress voted to pay Brady $25,000 for this collection.

These negatives were then entrusted to the War Department, where they were treated with indifference. Inquiries concerning the collection were abruptly turned aside. In August 1892, according to Jeana K. Foley, writing in *Mathew Brady and the Image of History*, Brady himself, approaching his seventieth birthday, wrote to the secretary of war to ask permission to make prints from the negatives, "the very negatives he had sold to the government," Foley points out. Brady's request was brusquely denied.

In 1897, a year after Brady's death, the War Department published the first catalog of the collection. Entitled *Subject Catalog No. 5: List of Photographic Negatives Relating to the War for the Union,* it listed and briefly described the 6,000 negatives.

In 1940, the collection was transferred to the National Archives. It is now stored at the Archives's research complex at College Park, Maryland. The photographs in this book are drawn mostly from these two Brady collections.

In making the switchover of photographic images from Library of Congress and National Archives collections to the pages of this book, a good number of archivists and curators helped me. Specialists at the Prints and Photographs Division of the Library of Congress were especially helpful. These include Mary Ison, head of the reference section, Beverly Brannan and Carol Johnson, both photograph curators, and Maya Keech, reference specialist.

Holly Reed, an archives specialist at the National Archives and Records Administration, and Jeana K. Foley, a specialist in photographs at the Smithsonian Institution, were also particulary helpful.

Athena Angelos, a professional pictorial researcher based in Washington, D.C., was indispensable in scanning and transferring to CDs each of the several hundred images that appear in the book. Patrick Falci, a former president of the Civil War Round Table of New York played a vital role in vetting the manuscript. Bill Sullivan acted as a translator.

Ann Shumard, Curator of Photographs at the National Portrait Gallery; Daile Kaplan, Vice President and Director of Photographs at the Swann Gallery in New York City; Sal Alberti and Jim Lowe, James Lowe Autographs, Mary Panzer, Thomas Harris and Ellen LiBretto were always generous with information and advice.

I owe special thanks to all of these individuals. The book would not have been possible without them.

1 Mathew Brady and His Legacy

Mathew Brady was approaching his fortieth birthday and at the peak of his fame as America's foremost photographer when the Civil War erupted in April 1861. Because of his often acclaimed skill and abundant success as a celebrity portraitist, and by virtue of the fashionable galleries that he operated in New York and Washington, D.C., true urban attractions, Brady had managed to spring from his farm-boy beginnings in upstate New York to become regarded as a person of prominence. All was not serene, however. Because he enjoyed spending money freely, Brady had overextended himself financially and many of his creditors had begun to harass him. The decision he made to photograph and sell Civil War scenes to the public may have been made, at least in part, in an effort to increase his income and stabilize his shaky finances.

Very early in his career, well before the Civil War, Brady had set out to accumulate the photographic portraits of the nation's rich and famous. He had achieved that goal. Through the years, American presidents, noted statesmen, lawyers, physicians, great writers and actors, and prominent women went before his cameras.

He reached into every aspect of American life for his subjects. He also photographed explorers and members of the clergy, revolutionaries and theatrical stars, American Indians and P. T. Barnum's midgets.

His subjects included visiting royalty and when royalty wasn't available, he photographed royal painted portraits—of Queen Victoria and Prince Albert, Alexander II, Emperor of Russia, Francis II, King of Naples, and scores of others—and made prints of the photos to sell.

Brady was very canny about what he did. People of note were granted free sittings. In one of his ledgers, clients identified as congressmen, senators, or judges often had "complimentary" written after their names.

Brady did not photograph celebrities simply to help assure his own fame, nor was profit his chief motive. He did it, he said, as a kind of public service; he did it to create a historical record. While Brady is usually remembered for his Civil War photographs, his collection of thousands of portraits made before the war is at least of equal importance in assessing what he was able to achieve.

When the Civil War broke out, Brady looked upon the event as a photographic historian. He hatched plans to send photographers to "all parts of the army." Each would travel in a horse-drawn wagon that would serve as a darkroom and storehouse for equipment and supplies. Brady's wife and some of his friends did not like the idea. But Brady had his mind made up and, much later, in a newspaper interview, he noted that " … destiny overruled me

Mathew Brady, *c.* 1856. Unidentified photographer

by saying, like Euphorion, I felt that I had to go. A spirit in my feet said 'Go' and I went."

"Is it too much to credit Brady with being one of the foremost historians of the day?" asked Robert Taft in *Photography and the American Scene*. "Not a conventional one to be sure, but one who deserves a place with a [George] Bancroft or a [William] Prescott." He was, as author James Horan called him, "a historian with a camera."

For someone so well known, Brady's origins are unusually obscure. He was probably born in 1823, although there are no records to document that fact. "I go back to 1823–24," he said during a newspaper interview when he was in his sixties. He noted that "my birthplace was Warren County, N.Y., in the woods about Lake George . . ." Warren County historians have pinpointed Johnsburg as Brady's place of birth.

"My father was an Irishman," Brady once recalled. The family had emigrated from Ireland not long before Mathew was born. Andrew, his father, was a farmer. His name first appears in the Warren County census records in 1830,

Mathew Brady, 1861. Brady studio

wherein the Bradys are listed as a family of two adults and six children.

As a teenager, Brady met artist William Page in Saratoga, New York, and received art instruction from him. Page later traveled to New York City, Brady claimed, and there was a pupil in an art class conducted by Samuel F. B. Morse, the portrait painter who was to become known as the inventor of the telegraph. Brady joined Page in New York.

A remarkable set of coincidences served to introduce Brady to photography. In 1839, Morse had been in Paris to demonstrate his telegraph to the Academy of Sciences. While there, he met Louis Daguerre, who had invented a process of forming a highly detailed image on a sheet of silver-coated copper. The images came to be called daguerreotypes. Morse had seen examples of Daguerre's work in the Frenchman's own studio. He found them to be "exquisite" and called the process "one of the most beautiful discoveries of the age."

Morse had a camera built for him, and when he returned to the United States and his post as a professor at the University of the City of New York (now New York University), he began taking experimental daguerreotypes. As Brady recalled, "He [Morse] had a loft in his brother's structure at Nassau and Beekman streets, with a telegraph stretched and embryo camera also at work." Brady claimed "I was introduced to Morse," and was later "counseled" in the art of daguerreotypy by a pair of chemists, both colleagues of Morse's, Professors John William Draper, the first president of the American Photographical Society, and Robert Ogden Doremus.

Despite the knowledge he had acquired, Brady did not enter the photographic field right away. Daguerreotypy was largely a novelty. For an entrepreneur, it was not an attractive field. Brady became a department store clerk, taking a job with the A. T. Stewart Company. The year was 1839, according to Stephen N. Elias, Alexander Stewart's biographer.

Stewart himself, one the wealthiest New Yorkers of his day, enjoyed a brilliant and innovative career as a retailer. He was one of the first merchants to mark prices on his goods rather than compel customers to haggle with sales clerks. He often offered quality goods at reduced prices and was advertising his one-price policy and special sales a decade before R. H. Macy and other retailers began to do so. According to one of his senior managers, as quoted by Elias, Stewart "outgeneraled every one of his contemporaries." Brady, once he had decided upon a career path, would do the same.

It is not clear how long Brady remained in his first job. But in 1843, in the New York City business and residence directory, he was listed as being in business for himself as a manufacturer of jewelry cases. Before long he was also turning out cases for surgical instruments and the leather-covered wooden cases in which daguerreotypes were enclosed. In a letter dated June 17, 1843, to Albert Southworth of the team of Southworth and (Josiah) Hawes, brilliant Boston daguerrians, Brady solicited the firm's business. "I have been engaged some time past," he writes in his letter, now in the possession of the International Museum of Photography at the George Eastman House, "in manufacturing miniature cases for some of the principal operators in this city and recently in business for myself and anxious for encouragement. I have got up a new type style case with embossed top and extra fine frame."

In 1844, Brady decided to open his own studio, what he called his "Daguerrian Miniature Gallery." He picked out a site on the west side of Broadway at the corner of Fulton Street. It was a bustling, thoroughly integrated neighborhood of what was fast becoming a great modern city.

The population grew at an exceptional rate during Brady's first decades in the city. In 1840, when Brady was clerking for A. T. Stewart, the population of New York and its boroughs stood at 391,114. By 1860, with the Civil War looming, it had risen to 1,174,479.

A large number of New York's citizens were immigrants, chiefly Irish Catholics and German Catholics. Their attempt to live and work in a city whose roots were Protestant and Anglo-Saxon led to ethnic animosity. The tension reached a peak with the Draft Riots during the summer of 1863. For four days, working-class whites ran wild, their anger stoked by the inequalities of the new draft law and the fear of losing their jobs to a mass of freed slaves who would, it was imagined, descend upon the city.

Despite his roots, Brady followed a policy of noninvolvement and sought to avoid strife in any way possible. In his profession, he always sought customers at the upper end of the economic scale. In his personal life, he preferred the company of artists and politicians. If he ever identified himself with the poor and struggling elements of New York's population, or sought to aid their cause, there is no evidence of it.

The Wall Street area to the south of Brady's studio was already the city's financial district. Other businesses had established themselves to the north: tinsmiths, engravers, and purveyors of dry goods. To the west, close to the commercial waterfront, were hotels, boardinghouses, ship chandlers, coopers, rope and cord merchants, stables, grocers, tobacconists, and working-class saloons.

Brady's studio at 205 Broadway, New York City, "View From the American Museum." Woodcut by unidentified artist, 1847–52

Mathew Brady, *c.* 1861

Across Fulton Street stood St. Paul's Church, centerpiece of the oldest parish in Manhattan. Astor House, New York's most exclusive hotel, was just beyond the church. At six stories and with 600 beds, Astor House was bigger than any hotel in Europe. Just to the north was City Hall and its spacious park.

Diagonally across Broadway from Brady's establishment, Phineas T. Barnum operated the American Museum. The man who would be hailed as "America's Greatest Showman" entertained his patrons with a continuous string of sideshows, minstrels, freaks, performing animals, beauty pageants, and fat-baby contests. Through the years, scores of exotic performers employed by Barnum would make their way across Broadway to be photographed at Brady's studio.

At first, Brady occupied only the top floor of the building at 205 Broadway. He had openings cut in the roof to accommodate skylights for admitting daylight. He may have been the first photographer to employ this approach in lighting subjects to be photographed.

Mathew Brady's studio at 359 Broadway, New York City. Woodcut engraving from *New York Illustrated News*, November 12, 1853

Brady patrons who climbed the three flights of stairs to the studio were often greeted by the proprietor himself and ushered into a chair before the camera lens. But it was not likely to be Brady who took the photograph. A childhood disease, once described by Brady as an "inflammation of the eyes," had left him with diminished eyesight and prevented him from getting a lens into sharp focus.

This scarcely inhibited him, however. Brady, like many other gallery owners of the time, employed "operators" to insert the prepared plate into the camera, focus the image on the ground glass, and remove the lens cap for the proper number of seconds to make the image.

Like Alexander Stewart, who hired the finest business talent, Brady sought out the best operators available and paid them the highest salaries. His gallery crew also included laboratory technicians who prepared the small rectangles of silver-plated copper for the camera by washing each in a solution of nitric acid, then exposing it to iodine vapor to make it sensitive to light.

After the image had been recorded on the plate and removed from the camera, it had to be exposed to mercury vapor until the portrait became visible. Then the image was "fixed" by immersing the plate in a bath of hyposulfite of soda. There were other assistants, who were responsible for mounting and framing images. There were colorists to enhance the hues of a subject's face. There were clerks to book appointments and send out bills.

Brady himself was an impresario. He was the manager; he was the director. He was there to welcome clients and make them feel comfortable and undoubtedly he assisted in posing individuals and groups. He did the hiring and firing. He was the marketing and advertising manager.

Brady's skillfully lighted portraits, simple and straightforward, usually displayed a heroic quality. A reviewer for *Spirit of the Times* in 1846 praised Brady's portraits as being "brilliantly clear and beautiful," and said that they boasted a quality of lighting and coloring that "surpasses anything we have seen in daguerreotypes."

Brady also acquired daguerreotypes made by other photographers, copied them, and then sold the copies under his own name. Celebrity daguerreotypes, whether copies or Brady originals, sold for several times as much as an ordinary portrait.

From the very beginning, Brady was concerned with the social and professional status of those who sat for him. He sought to make portraits of the most distinguished and notable citizens of the day. Before long, his gallery had become a kind Hall of Fame where visitors could view the faces of American luminaries. Daniel Webster, Henry Clay, and James Fenimore Cooper were among his early subjects. At the time, the faces of notable Americans were known to the public only through paintings, lithographs, or engravings. The images recorded by the Brady cameramen thus had an awesome quality to them. Thousands flocked to see them.

James K. Polk, one of some seventeen presidents that Brady would photograph, was the first to pose for his camera in the White House.

In a diary entry for February 14, 1849, Polk wrote: "I yielded to the request of an artist named Brady of New York by sitting for my daguerreotype likeness today. I sat in the large dining room."

Lincoln was a frequent subject of Brady's. In their book *Lincoln in Photographs: An Album of Every Known Pose,* Lloyd Ostendorf and Charles Hamilton credited Brady with taking eleven Lincoln photographs (of the approximately 130 known to exist). Another two dozen were taken by cameramen employed by Brady, often at the Washington, D.C., studio.

The business of professional daguerreotypy grew dramatically during the late 1840s and the 1850s. In *The American Daguerreotype*, Floyd and Marion Rinhart call the growth of daguerreotypy at this time "enormous," with the number of studios increasing from sixteen in 1844 to fifty-nine in 1850. With the galleries concentrated along Broadway between Fulton and Canal Streets. There were also firms that manufactured and sold the chemicals and equipment necessary for making daguerreotypes.

New York also became a center for articles and books on photography. As early as 1847, the enterprising John Plumbe, Jr., an early franchiser who founded daguerreotype studios in New York, Boston, Philadelphia, and Baltimore, produced the National Plumbeotype Gallery, a collection of twenty-seven portraits of national figures. Each was made by copying a daguerreotype on a lithographic stone, and then printing lithographs from it. Henry Hunt Snelling's *The History and Practice of the Art of Photography* made its appearance in 1849. A trade paper, *The Daguerrian Journal*, began to be published in 1850.

In 1850, Brady took on a role pioneered by Plumbe. He produced what he called "The Gallery of Illustrious Americans," a collection of lithographs by Francis D'Avignon, one of the finest portrait lithographers of the day. Copied from Brady's daguerreotypes, each lithographic portrait was the size of a tabloid newspaper page. As originally planned, twenty-four of "the most eminent citizens of the American public" were to be included in the collection.

Mathew Brady with wife, Juliette Handy, and Mrs. Haggerty. Daguerreotype, *c.* 1860. Brady studio

Because of a lack of public interest in the project, the number was reduced to twelve. These included two presidents, Zachary Taylor and Millard Fillmore, two generals, John C. Frémont and Winfield Scott, and such political stalwarts as Daniel Webster, Henry Clay, and John C. Calhoun. While the project was not a financial success, it added to Brady's prestige.

Like so many important events of Brady's life, the facts surrounding his marriage are obscure. His bride was Juliette Handy, known as Julia. The couple was married probably in 1851. There is no marriage record, but newspapers of that date report the Bradys traveling in Europe in 1851, where they remained for almost a year. During his absence, Brady assigned George Cook, an able and experienced daguerreotypist, to manage his gallery.

The same year, the Great Exhibition in London's stunning new Crystal Palace took place. One of the exhibits was devoted to photography. The Bradys, on their grand tour of Europe, stopped in London for the fair, where Brady exhibited forty-eight daguerreotypes.

Photographers from five other countries also displayed their work. Three of the five grand prizes went to American photographers, including one to Brady for his overall mastery of the daguerreotype medium.

By the time the Bradys returned to New York, a wet-collodion process of photography on glass had been announced. It was soon to replace the daguerreotype and all other methods of producing pictures. The process involved pouring syrupy collodion onto a clean glass plate. When the collodion had set but not dried, the plate was bathed in a solution of silver nitrate to sensitize it. The still wet plate was then inserted into a holder and the holder placed in the camera so the plate could be exposed. After, the plate was developed, washed, and the image fixed. The result was a negative on glass from which any number of prints could be made.

When undertaken at a location that was remote from a studio, as during the Civil War, the work was difficult and demanding. Normally, two photographers would be involved.

They worked in the cramped space of a canopy covered wagon. It was dark and smelly, and in the summer temperatures reached 100 degrees and beyond. When a photograph was to be taken, chemicals were mixed and a glass plate prepared. Placed in a holder, the plate would be inserted in a camera that had already been positioned and focused on the subject. The exposure of the plate and the development of the image had to be completed within a very few minutes; otherwise, there could be a loss of intensity and tonal quality in the print.

Brady had always admired daguerreotypes for their beauty and uniqueness and resisted switching over to the wet-plate process for a time. But the fact that the glass-plate process was cheaper and produced a negative that could be used in producing multiple paper copies assured its success.

Brady quickly raised the production of paper prints to new heights by creating portraits of enormous size, as large as 17 by 21 inches. The subtle sepia tones of these poster-like images would be skillfully retouched with India inks and even oil paints to create what looked to be a fine portrait. "Brady Imperials," he called them. Each sold from fifty to hundred dollars and up.

To produce Imperials, Brady hired a new operator named Alexander Gardner, who was skilled in the wet-plate process and in the operation of the large-plate camera used to produce the over-size prints. From Scotland, the 35-year-old Gardner had emigrated to the United States in 1856, the same year he went to work for Brady. He had previously worked as a jeweler, newspaper publisher, and secretary for a project that sought to establish a utopian community in Iowa.

Gardner was experienced in bookkeeping and a good businessman. When Brady opened a gallery in Washington, D.C. in 1858, he sent Gardner to run it. Brady remained in New York. Gardner proved to be an astute manager and before long the gallery was operating at a profit.

But Brady and Gardner disagreed over policy. One of their differences concerned *cartes de visite*. These small card photographs, measuring

2½ by 4 inches, and usually with a portrait on the front, had become enormously popular. Available not only at photographers' studios, but also at newsstands, bookstores, and print shops, *cartes de visite* often carried portraits of heroes and leaders of the past and present. Pictures of family members were also rendered in *cartes-de-visite* size. Virtually every home had an album containing their favorites.

Gardner recognized *cartes de visite* to be a fine way of boosting the Washington gallery's profits. To help mass-produce the small cards, he developed a four-lens camera that could make four images on a single glass plate, thus quadrupling the number of pictures that could be made at one time. Brady, however, looked down upon the little cards, which were sold for between ten and twenty-five cents apiece. They required no great skill on the part of the camera operator and were too small to allow for elaborate retouching. Brady favored Imperials and the high prices they fetched.

Since Brady's galleries were not prepared to meet the surging demand for *cartes*, Gardner suggested that Brady enter into a contract with E. and H. T. Anthony of New York, the largest photographic supply company in the country, to produce and distribute the small photographs from negatives supplied by Brady. Under the terms of the contract eventually agreed upon, Brady began to receive about $4,000 a year in royalty payments from the Anthony firm.

During this period, the late 1850s and early 1860s, paper prints from glass negatives were also being used to create stereographs. Made with a special double-lens camera that produced two slightly different images of the same subject, each stereograph, when viewed through a hand-held optical instrument known as a stereoscope, gave the effect of three dimensions.

The Civil War would sharply boost the demand for stereographs. In depicting any type of image, they provided much more drama and excitement than a single photograph. Their popularity continued into the twentieth century.

In 1864, in the midst of the stereograph and *cartes de visite* craze, Brady opened a new and more elaborate studio at Broadway and Tenth

opposite page:
Mathew Brady's studio, Broadway
and Tenth St., New York, *c.* 1864

Interior view, Mathew Brady's
studio, Broadway and Tenth St.,
New York. Engraving from *Frank
Leslie's Illustrated Newspaper,* 1861.
Artist unidentified

Brady's stereo camera.
George Eastman House,
International Museum of Photography

Street, across Broadway from fashionable Grace Church and a huge new department store being erected by Alexander Stewart. *Leslie's* hailed the gallery for its "costly carpet … elegant and luxurious couches … and artistic gas fixtures." Brady also provided a private entrance for ladies arriving in evening dress, "to obviate," as *Leslie's* noted, "the unpleasant necessity of passing, so attired, through the public gallery."

About a month after its lavish grand opening, the gallery was the scene of what Brady himself felt was one of the paramount events of his career. The eighteen-year-old Prince of Wales, Albert Edward, the youngest son of Queen Victoria, paid a royal visit to Canada and the United States. As the first member of the British royal family to visit America, the prince awoke great curiosity and excitement wherever he went. A half a million New Yorkers turned out to welcome him. A torchlight procession, a grand ball, plus services at Trinity Church were held in the prince's honor.

Brady made a formal request that the prince and his entourage visit his new gallery—and the prince accepted the invitation. During the visit, which lasted two to three hours, the prince and those accompanying him sat for individual and group portraits and spent time gazing upon Brady's photographs of notable Americans. Afterward, according to *The New York Times*, they "complimented Mr. Brady highly upon his proficiency and art."

Brady later recalled speaking with the Duke of Newcastle, who was in charge of the event's logistics. "Your Grace," said Brady, "might I ask to what I owe your favor to my studio."

"Are you not the Mr. Brady who earned the prize nine years ago in London? You owe it to yourself. We had your place of business down in our notebooks before we started."

Despite his exalted social status and the fact that he operated what appeared to be popular galleries in New York and Washington, Brady's finances were in a troubled state. He had always lived high, dressing in fancy clothes and traveling often. Equipping and furnishing the Tenth Street gallery, and providing for an extravagant opening, had cost him a small fortune.

According to *Leslie's*, as quoted by Barbara Mc-Candless, assistant curator of photographs at the Amon Carter Museum, writing in *Photography in the Twentieth Century*, Brady at the time "could buy only for cash and did not pay well."

As 1861 began, one Southern state after another left the Union to join the Confederacy and the nation edged closer and closer to war. Young men in both the North and South rushed to enter the armies. Brady, with thoughts of covering the war, may have had a financial motivation, seeing the conflict as an opportunity "to recover what he had lost in earlier ventures," so states Barbara McCandless.

Brady made the first of his Civil War photographs early in July 1861 in and around Washington. According to historian Josephine Cobb, a one-time specialist in charge of Civil War photographs at the National Archives, these were photographs of military units that included the Twelfth New York Regiment at Camp Anderson and the First Rhode Island Regiment at Camp Sprague. Throughout the war, Brady would continue to concentrate on photographs of this type, that is, those depicting military units. In her book *Mathew Brady and the Image of History*, Mary Panzer writes "fully three-quarters [of Brady's images] are devoted to the representation of individuals, groups, and regiments."

Brady, along with a handful of other Washington-based photographers, sought to cover the first engagement of the Civil War, the Battle of Bull Run (or First Manassas), that took place not far from Washington in mid-July 1861. It was a stunning defeat for the Federals, whose retreat turned into a headlong flight back to the capital. Commenting on Brady's attempt to record the event, *The New York Times* noted: "On the disastrous day of Bull Run, he [Brady] stood upon the field with camera and chemicals, and would have photographed the retreat had it not been conducted with too much rapidity." No photographs were made that day, or at least none has ever come to light.

A series of photographs from Antietam also added to the Brady legend that was beginning to emerge. Taken by Alexander Gardner and

James Gibson, both of whom were employed at the time, they featured startling views of battlefield dead. The images made a lasting impression on the many hundreds of New Yorkers who crowded into Brady's gallery to look at them. But Gardner and Gibson received no credit. The photographs were identified as being the work of Brady and hailed by the press as such.

Brady moved to Washington in 1861 to supervise operations at his gallery there and direct his coverage of the war. Alexander Gardner had the gallery running smoothly. Photographs had been taken of the new president, Abraham Lincoln, his wife, members of his cabinet, and key members of the House and Senate. Sales of *cartes de visite* were proving profitable. Gardner may have resented Brady's intrusion. In the words of Josephine Cobb, Gardner "became restive." The fact that Brady routinely took credit for photographs Gardner had taken may also have irked the Scotsman. Late in 1862 or early in 1863, Gardner parted company with Brady and decided to start photographing the

"Brady the Photographer Returned from Bull Run."
July 22, 1861. Photographer unidentified

Mathew Brady at McPherson's Woods, Gettysburg. July 15, 1863. Brady studio

Mathew Brady (standing, at right), with cameraman and assistants. Berlin (now Brunswick), MD, October 28, 1862

"Court House [sic] or City Hall," Yorktown, VA, with (possibly) Mathew Brady at left. May 1862. Photographer unidentified

Civil War on his own. Two of Brady's best photographers, Timothy O'Sullivan and James Gibson, followed Gardner and started working for him. Brady shrugged off these losses. He simply hired more cameramen.

The war was not very old when Brady decided he no longer wished to suffer the discomforts or expenses of attempting to cover battles in far-flung places. According to Josephine Cobb, a "better idea had come to him." Brady decided he would expand his collection of war views simply by obtaining the work of other photographers. He began to borrow negatives from his colleagues or exchange images with them. When a photographer made more than one exposure of a scene, Brady would purchase the "second" from him.

He did more. When he obtained a print from another photographer, he would make a copy negative from it. The prints he subsequently made from these negatives became part of his collection.

In l866, Alexander Gardner would publish *Gardner's Photographic Sketch Book of the War*, a two-volume work that contained some one hundred of the best photographs that he had taken during the war. The same year, George Barnard's *Photographic Views of Sherman's Campaign* was released. Brady copied the photographs from both of these volumes, which were to become classics. While he did not make it a point of claiming to have photographed these views, many of them eventually became associated with the Brady name.

Through much of his career, Brady enhanced his reputation through a cozy relationship with what is now called the print media. His association with *Frank Leslie's Illustrated Newspaper* and *Harper's Weekly*, the popular illustrated newspapers of the time, was especially valuable. *Leslie's* began operation in 1855; *Harper's* arrived in 1857. In its very first issue, *Leslie's* featured a wood engraving on page one that had been copied from a Brady photograph, with appropriate credit for Brady. In the years that followed, both *Leslie's* and *Harper's* relied heavily on engravings made from Brady images. Such illustrations frequently carried

General Ambrose E. Burnside (reading newspaper), with Mathew Brady at Army of the Potomac Headquarters, Cold Harbor, VA. June 11/12, 1864. Photographer unidentified

the credit line: "From Photograph by Brady." Thus Brady was in the forefront of this early form of photojournalism. Photographs themselves did not become widely used in newspapers until the dawn of the halftone era the 1880s.

Several times during the war, *The New York Times* spoke of Brady, using almost reverential terms. After Antietam, for example, the *Times*, in an editorial, noted: "From the outset of the war, Mr. Brady has been in the field. His cameras have followed the cannon from the Potomac to the York, from the Chesapeake to the Alleghenies. Scarcely has been the camp of volunteers been pitched by the more or less muddy waters of the Chickahominy ere the patriotic Polyphemus plants himself within range, flings away his green curtain, and opens his one-eyed battery upon the scene. Like the sunlight, which he presses into his service and ours, this silent Asmodeus penetrates into every secret, unveils every mystery."

Brady also came to be identified in the public's mind with the Civil War through his fondness for posing before his own cameras at battle sites. In the summer of 1861, he was photographed in connection with Bull Run (the date and the name of the battle were scratched into the negative, so they would appear on each print) and at Harper's Ferry in 1862. Brady photographers continued to cover their employer each year for the rest of the war. At Petersburg and Richmond near the war's end, Brady's cameramen documented his presence with great frequency.

Other photographers preferred to remain behind the camera. Photographs of Alexander Gardner and Timothy O'Sullivan are very rare. Of James Gibson, there seem to be none at all.

Brady was much more of a success in making a name for himself than in earning a profit. The

"Gentlemen's Committee on the Fine Arts for the Metropolitan Fair in Aid of the u.s. Sanitary Commission," with Mathew Brady (seated in center), 1864. Photographer unidentified

General Robert B. Potter and staff, with Mathew Brady at far right. Petersburg, (probably) June 21, 1864. Photographer unidentified

Cowan's 1st New York Battery, Jordan's Farm, Petersburg, with Mathew Brady at far left, June 20, 1864. Photographer unidentified

Mathew Brady's photo wagon at Petersburg, with (possibly) David Woodbury seated at center, *c.* 1864

Pratt's Castle, Gambler's Hill, with Mathew Brady (center). Richmond, VA, April 1865

sales of Brady's war views, which he hoped would provide a substantial income, were a disappointment. Meanwhile, Brady's expenditures for photographic equipment and chemicals kept mounting. Brady, like most Northerners, had believed that the war was going to be a short one. But when it dragged on and on, with battles often occurring at places far removed from Washington, Brady found it increasingly difficult to support his crews of photographers and their traveling darkrooms.

Well before the war ended, Brady's financial situation had become desperate. He could no longer pay his photographers' salaries. He could not afford photographic supplies or even meet his rent payments. The crush of nonpayment suits filed against Brady forced him into bankruptcy, first in Washington in 1864, and later in New York.

After the Civil War, most of the photographers who had covered the conflict went on to other ventures. Alexander Gardner became chief photographer for the Union Pacific Rail Way and helped launch an era of Western land-scape photography. Timothy O'Sullivan did much the same, serving as an expeditionary photographer for a full decade. Brady, however, turned his back on such enterprises. Instead, he campaigned to sell his vast collection of portraits and Civil War views. He first tried the New-York Historical Society. When that effort failed, he turned to the federal government.

His many debts weighed heavily upon him. He found himself unable to pay the rent on the warehouse space where he had stored thousands of his glass negatives. The government bought the negatives for $2,500, setting off a chain of events leading to legislation passed by Congress in 1875 providing for a payment of $25,000 to Brady for "a perfect title" to the negatives.

Brady was able to pay his debts but his problems were not solved. He had lost his New York gallery and various real estate investments he had made. He eventually lost his Washington studio, too. In the last years of his life, he was poor, painfully ill with arthritis, and, after the death of his wife in 1887, lonely. Brady died in 1896 in a New York hospital following a streetcar accident. He was seventy-two.

Josephine Cobb once noted that "to the day of his death" Brady remained confident that his portraits of notable Americans and his Civil War photographs would be published by the government as soon as the technology had been developed that would provide for fine reproduction. And he had no doubt that his war photos would come to be acclaimed for providing a reliable history of the conflict. "There is no collection like it in the country, or the world," he once said.

Brady was prescient on both counts. Thanks to his efforts in compiling a "National Portrait Gallery," as he called it, the nation has a visual record of many hundreds of famous faces of the nineteenth century. Because he encouraged and organized the photographic coverage of the Civil War from the beginning to the very end, then kept his vast accumulation of photographs relatively intact, he gave subsequent generations a stunning visual record of what the war was like.

Decade after decade, Brady's photographs turn up everywhere. They are used to illustrate articles and essays, textbooks and trade books, and every type of nonfiction television presentation. Brady's Civil War-period photographs of Abraham Lincoln were used to create the Lincoln portraits that appear on the five-dollar bill and penny and are hailed as the most reproduced works of art in history.

Mathew Brady did what he set out to do. In *Mathew Brady and the Image of History*, Jeana K. Foley cites, a *Washington Post* article that quoted Brady as saying, "My greatest aim has been to advance the art [of photography] and to make it what I think I have, a great and truthful medium of history." He surely would have been pleased with the way things turned out.

Mathew Brady, *c.* 1889.
Brady studio (possibly).
Levin Handy, photographer

2   The First Battle of Bull Run (Manassas)

The first major battle of the Civil War took place only about thirty miles from Washington, D.C., along the south bank of Bull Run, a quiet creek north of Manassas, Virginia. (The battle is also known as the First Manassas.) Fought on July 21, 1861, a Sunday, it was not a battle in the usual sense of the word but more a collision of opposing masses of untrained amateur soldiers.

General Irwin McDowell commanded the Federal army. His 35,000 men were "green," as Lincoln described them. Hurriedly recruited in the North for three months of service, their terms of enlistment were about to expire when they were ordered into action.

McDowell was ordered to attack the 22,000 Confederates, also "green," under General Pierre G. T. Beauregard and drive them from the important railroad junction at Manassas.

Another 12,000 Confederate troops, commanded by General Joseph E. Johnston, were posted at Winchester at the southern end of the Shenandoah Valley. A second Federal army, under General Robert Patterson, had been posted in front of Johnston to prevent his army from joining Beauregard's. But Johnston managed to slip past Patterson and link up with Beauregard at Manassas before McDowell arrived.

The fighting began when McDowell ordered an attack against Beauregard's left flank. For a time it appeared as if the Federal troops might break through the Southern line. But the arrival of fresh Confederates helped to turn the tide. McDowell passed the word to retreat. While the withdrawal began in orderly fashion, it turned into a rout as soldiers and their officers got mixed up with civilians who had come out from Washington to see the show. Some of them had brought picnic baskets.

McDowell's defeat sent shock waves through the North. Many had believed that the war would be over quickly, perhaps in a matter of weeks. Bull Run was a dose of reality. Northerners came to realize that a long struggle lay ahead.

Brady began his photographic coverage of the Civil War at Bull Run. In a newspaper interview in 1891, Brady said, "I went to the first battle of Bull Run with two wagons from Washington. My personal companions were Dick McCormick, then a newspaper writer, Ned House, and Al Waud, the sketch artist. We stayed all night at Centreville; we got as far as Blackburne's Ford, we made pictures and expected to be in Richmond the next day, but it was not so, and our apparatus was a good deal damaged on the way back to Washington ...."

Eleven days after the battle, an article appeared in the *American Journal of Photography* that confirmed Brady's misfortune. Brady, the article said, got as far as the "smoke of Bull Run and was aiming his never failing tube at friends and foe alike when with the rest of our Grand Army they were completely routed and took to their heels, losing their photographic accoutrements on the ground, which the Rebels no doubt pounced upon as trophies of victory."

Timothy O'Sullivan is likely to have been at Bull Run, too. Perhaps he accompanied Brady to the battle site, for he suffered adversity similar to that of his employer. In an article in September 1869, *Harper's Monthly Magazine* noted that O'Sullivan was at the battle, and would have photographed events close-up "but for the fact that a shell from one of the rebel field-pieces took away the photographic camera."

While attempts were undoubtedly made to photograph at Bull Run in 1861, not a single photograph of the battle has ever been seen. Photographers did not produce any Bull Run photographs until the Confederate army evacuated the area in March 1862. George N. Barnard and James F. Gibson then moved in to take photographs of the battlefield, of housing erected by the Confederates, and various landmarks. Those photographs are represented on these pages.

View of the Battlefield. Bull Run, VA,
1862. Photographer unidentified

Federal cavalry at Sudley Ford. Bull Run,
VA, 1862. George Barnard, photographer

Manassas, VA. Confederate fortifications, with Federal soldiers, 1862. George Barnard, photographer

View of Bull Run. Bull Run, VA, 1862. Photographer unidentified

Sudley church. Bull Run, VA, 1862.
George Barnard, photographer

Centreville, VA. Fort on heights, with
Quaker guns, 1862. George Barnard,
photographer

Matthews', or the Stone House. Bull Run, VA, 1862.
George Barnard, photographer

Manassas, VA. Confederate winter quarters, 1862.
Timothy O'Sullivan, photographer

3 Port Royal and Fort Pulaski

Less than a week after the firing at Fort Sumter, President Abraham Lincoln proclaimed a naval plan to close the ports of the Southern states that had seceded from the Union, preventing ships from entering or exiting them. Secretary of the Navy Gideon Welles was called upon to organize the blockade. Welles began immediately to find the ships necessary to get the blockade established, pressing into service almost anything that could float and carry a big gun.

It took time for the blockade to succeed. Getting the ships wasn't the only obstacle. Supplying and repairing the blockading vessels was another problem. Ships stationed along the Atlantic coast had to return to bases at Hampton Roads, Virginia, or Key West, Florida, for resupply, which sometimes meant many hundreds of miles of ocean travel. Some vessels spent more time underway than in actual blockade duty.

To solve the problem, Welles decided the best course of action would be to establish Federal bases along the Confederate coast. Late in August 1861, a squadron of seven naval vessels commanded by Flag Officer Silas Stringham, along with transports bearing an infantry company General Benjamin Butler, launched an assault on the Confederate forts that guarded Hatteras Inlet, North Carolina. Stringham's bombardment from his huge steam frigates quickly forced the Confederates to surrender, giving the Union a base of operations on the North Carolina coast.

A more ambitious sea-and-land expedition under Union Brigadier General Thomas W. Sherman (the other Sherman) and Navy Captain

Samuel F. Du Pont that consisted of seventeen wooden cruisers and about 12,000 men put to sea on November 7, 1861. Their plan was to attack the Hilton Head-Port Royal area, in South Carolina between Savannah, Georgia, and Charleston. Du Pont lost no time in shelling Forts Walker and Beauregard into submission and occupying Port Royal, gaining the Federals another important base for coaling and supplying the blockading fleet.

Operations in the area did not end with the seizure of Port Royal. Early in March 1862, Federal forces ranged south, occupying Fernandina, Florida. Fort Pulaski, Georgia, on an island near the mouth of the Savannah River, and which protected the harbor of Savannah, Georgia, was taken during the second week in April. Fort Macon, protecting the approach to Beaufort, South Carolina, was also captured.

Timothy O'Sullivan was on hand when Du Pont's warships pounded Forts Walker and Beauregard. He was at Port Royal and Fort Pulaski. In March and April 1862, O'Sullivan traveled to Hilton Head and Beaufort, South Carolina. The photographs that O'Sullivan made at these battle sites represent the first successful efforts at photographic coverage of the Civil War.

Rear view of Fort Walker.
Hilton Head, sc, November 1861.
Timothy O'Sullivan, photographer

Dock built by Federal troops.
Hilton Head, sc, April 1862.
Timothy O'Sullivan, photographer

The Beauregard gun.
Fort Pulaski, GA, April 1862.
Timothy O'Sullivan, photographer

Dismounted mortar.
Fort Pulaski, GA, April 1862.
Timothy O'Sullivan, photographer

50th Pennsylvania Infantry in parade formation.
Beaufort, SC, February 1862.
Timothy O'Sullivan, photographer

Interior view. Fort Pulaski, GA, April 1862. Timothy O'Sullivan, photographer

The Breach. Fort Pulaski, GA, April 1862. Photographer unidentified

Coosaw Ferry, Port Royal Island, SC (In the distance, battleground of January 1, 1862), 1862. Timothy O'Sullivan, photographer

4 The Federal Navy

When the Civil War erupted, the U.S. Navy was well thought of as a deep-water navy, adequate for combat on the high seas. But it was ill trained and poorly equipped for what was to come, chiefly operations on inland rivers and the shallow waters off the Atlantic and Gulf coasts.

The Confederates had no navy at all. Under the energetic leadership of Secretary of the Navy Stephen Mallory, the South built several vessels that proved troublesome for the Federals and ordered sleek cruisers from the British that harassed the North's merchant shipping. The South, however, was sorely lacking in naval facilities and the resources to build ships, and thus unable to keep pace with the Federals, whose Navy became one of the world's most powerful.

Federal naval strategy at the outset of the war was dictated by the blockade. On April 19, 1861, less than a week after Fort Sumter had fallen to the Confederacy, President Lincoln announced that in order to protect "the public peace," he was ordering naval ships to be stationed outside all Confederate ports to prevent merchant vessels from entering or departing. Ships seeking to evade the blockade would be subject to inspection and seizure.

Lincoln had outlined an awesome task. The coastline to be blockaded covered some 3,500 miles, stretching from Maryland to Mexico. The Navy was also charged with the responsibility of controlling the Mississippi River all the way from Cairo, Illinois, to the Gulf of Mexico.

To whip the navy into shape for blockading duty, Lincoln called upon Gideon Welles, a

Connecticut lawyer and newspaper editor who had served as chairman of the state's delegation to the Republican National Convention of 1860, naming him Secretary of the Navy. Tall, with a flowing white beard and quaint brown wig, the shrewd and able Welles worked vigorously to build a navy suited for the job at hand. He was one of Lincoln's best cabinet appointments.

Like other navies of the world at the time, the u.s. Navy was in the midst of revolutionary change, with its ships making the transition from sail to steam. Steam power was not considered suitable for every type of vessel, however. Seagoing ships and others committed to very long voyages used steam merely as an auxiliary power source because of their enormous coal requirements combined with the scarcity of coaling stations.

The period of change had begun years before. As early as 1842, Congress had given a green light to the construction of the *Princeton*, the Navy's first steam and screw propeller warship. The vessel's engine and propeller were designed by John Ericsson, who later would win renown for his role in the design and construction of the *Monitor*. Although its power plant was capable of moving the ship through the water at good speed, the *Princeton* was built of wood and carried a full set of sails.

The Navy was well aware of a growing trend toward the construction of ironclad ships and also in 1842 prevailed upon Congress to authorize the construction of an ironclad steam warship, to be built by Robert L. Stevens of Hoboken, New Jersey. But because of design changes and Congress's refusal to provide sufficient funding for the project, the vessel was never completed.

At the start of the Civil War, the Federal Navy had some ninety warships. More than half of these were sailing vessels. About forty were steam driven. A great number were tied up at various navy yards and not ready for active duty, "out of commission," that is.

Six of the Navy's newest ships were powerful steam frigates with screw propellers. Besides their substantial power plants, these vessels were noted for their heavy armament. Each boasted forty 9-inch rifles on the gun decks, plus several larger weapons on the spar decks. All of these ships, however, were out of commission.

The *Merrimac* was the best known of the frigates. Captured by the Confederates after it had been abandoned by the Federals, the vessel became the first Confederate ironclad.

Twelve other of the Federal Navy's newer vessels were steam sloops with screw propellers. These were less powerful than the frigates but still regarded as decent battle ships. Interestingly, before approving the legislation calling for the construction of the Navy's steam sloops and frigates, Southern senators had made certain that the draft of these vessels would be so great that none would be able to enter a Southern harbor.

To enforce the blockade, Welles and his capable assistant, Gustavus J. Fox, searched port cities of the Atlantic coast for vessels that could be chartered or purchased and made to carry a few guns. Their quest resulted in a bizarre assortment of ferryboats, tugboats, excursion steamers, fishing and whaling vessel, and old clipper ships, all of which they assigned to blockade duty.

At the same time, Welles and Fox launched an aggressive construction program. Soon the shipyards of the North were turning out fast ocean cruisers and small steam-powered warships, built in such a short amount of time that they were sometimes referred to as "ninety-day gunboats." Within a year, Welles and Fox had added 300 vessels to the Federal fleet. At the war's end, the Union Navy numbered 671 vessels.

Shipboard armament during the war was heavily influenced by Captain John Dahlgren, "the father of American naval ordnance." Powerful "dahlgrens," as they were called, had an unusual shape. Instead of being tubelike in design, they were thicker at the breech, the rear part of the gun, so that they were somewhat bottle shaped. Dahlgrens of nine, ten, and eleven-inch bores were put in service aboard the Navy's new steam frigates. Some even larger guns—thirteen inchers—were also built. These could launch projectiles weighing as much as 280 pounds.

Lincoln enjoyed Dahlgren's company. He appointed him head of the Bureau of Ordnance and often visited Dahlgren at the Washington Navy Yard. When Dahlgren made known his preference for sea duty, he was named to take charge of Federal naval operations against Charleston.

Slowly, the blockade became effective. Although it never fully succeeded in halting foreign trade with the South, it caused serious shortages of food and clothing among the civilian population and deprived the military of much needed weapons and ammunition. In so doing, the blockade played a major role in crippling the South's war effort.

Gun crew on deck of a monitor. Unknown location, 1861–1865. Photographer unidentified

Federal screw sloop Pensacola. Alexandria, VA, 1861. James Gibson, photographer

Rear Admiral John A. Dahlgren on the deck of the
screw sloop Pawnee. Charleston Harbor, sc, 1860–
1865. Photographer unidentified

Officers of Federal monitor Catskill. Charleston
Harbor, sc, 1865. Photographer Unidentified

Howitzer on deck of Federal screw sloop Pawnee.
Charleston Harbor, sc, 1861–1865. Photographer
unidentified

Federal screw sloop Pawnee,
deck view. Charleston Harbor,
sc, 1861–1865. Photographer
unidentified

Rear Admiral David D. Porter aboard the Malvern, flagship of the North Atlantic blockading squadron. Hampton Roads, VA, December 1864. Photographer unidentified

Federal training ship Sabine. Hampton Roads, VA, December 1864. Photographer unidentified

Union steamer Fort Donelson,
former Confederate blockade runner
Robert E. Lee. Norfolk, VA, December 1864. Photographer unidentified

Destroyed buildings at Navy Yard.
Norfolk, VA, December 1864.
Alexander Gardner, photographer

Crew of Federal gunboat Mendota. James River, VA,
1863–1864. Photographer unidentified

Federal gunboat Mendota. James River, VA,
1863–1864. Photographer unidentified

Federal shallow-draft monitor Casco,
converted to a torpedo boat. James
River, VA, 1861–1865. Photographer
unidentified

Federal monitor Canonicus taking
on coal from a schooner.
James River, VA, 1861–1865.
Photographer unidentified

Bow of captured Confederate gunboat Teaser. James
River, VA, July 4. 1862. Photographer unidentified

Federal double-turret monitor Onondaga. James River,
VA, 1864. Photographer unidentified

74

B-5191

Federal transport State of Maine.
Unknown location, 1861–1865.
Photographer unidentified

Officers on deck of Federal screw
sloop Kearsarge, with Captain
John A. Winslow third from left.
Unknown location, 1861–1865.
Photographer unidentified

448

Federal sloop Karnak. Unknown location, 1864–1865. Photographer unidentified

Federal sloop Karnak, deck view. Unknown location, June 4, 1864. Photographer unidentified

Karnak
9 March 1864

QM-59

Federal monitor Mahopac. Appomattox River, VA, 1864. Photographer unidentified

Officers of Federal monitor Mahopac. Unknown location, 1861–1865. Photographer unidentified

Battered smokestack from the
Confederate ironclad ram Virginia
No. 2. Unknown location, 1861–
1865. Photographer unidentified

Ironworks on deck of a monitor.
Unknown location, 1861–1865.
Photographer unidentified

Federal transport Linda and
monitor. Deep Bottom, VA, 1864.
Photographer unidentified

Federal gunboat Fort Hindman,
Mississippi River fleet.
Unknown location, 1861–1865.
Photographer unidentified

Federal transports with cargoes of artillery. Drewry's
Bluff, VA, April 1865. Photographer unidentified

Federal river steamer Kingston. Unknown location,
1861–1865. Photographer unidentified

86

QM-62

Federal gunboat General Grant. Unidentified location, 1861–1865. Photographer unidentified

Federal transport steamer Wauhatchee. Unknown location, 1861–1865. Photographer unidentified

Crew of Federal Army gunboat General Foster ashore with howitzers. Point of Rocks, VA, 1861–1865. Photographer unidentified

Former Confederate ironclad ram Stonewall. Off Washington, DC, 1865. Photographer unidentified

Officers of Federal transport Philadelphia. Unknown location, 1861–1865. Photographer unidentified

5   The Battle of the Ironclads

On March 8, 1862, the *Merrimac*, the first Confederate ironclad, steamed down the Elizabeth River toward Norfolk and Hampton Roads, a blue water channel at the mouth of the James River. The crew thought the ship was out for a test run. But Flag Officer Franklin Buchanan, who had been named the *Merrimac*'s captain, had other ideas, and gave orders for the vessel to attack the Federal Navy's wooden blockaders that were stationed at the harbor's entrance.

After ramming the *Cumberland* and causing it to go down, the *Merrimac* destroyed the *Congress* and then forced the *Minnesota* to run aground. Fire from the Federal warships deflected harmlessly off the *Merrimac*'s armored hull. At dusk, the *Merrimac* left the battle scene and returned to its anchorage. Buchanan

planned to return the next day and finish off the *Minnesota*.

Early on the morning of March 9, as the *Merrimac* approached the crippled *Minnesota*, its crew became distracted by a third vessel, one that resembled a long floating raft with a revolving gun turret on top. Within the turret were two 11-inch guns. The vessel was the *Monitor*.

The *Merrimac* was a rebuilt ship, a wooden frigate that had been abandoned and scuttled by the Federals, then salvaged by the Confederates and sheathed with iron plates. (*Merrimack* – with a "k" – was the official name of the vessel, but in common usage the "k" was dropped. People also used the term *Merrimac* more frequently than *Virginia*, the name the ship received at its rechristening.) The *Monitor*, on the other hand, had been designed and built under the supervision of John Ericsson, a brilliant Swedish engineer, at a Brooklyn, New York shipyard.

The two vessels hammered away at one another for several hours. The *Merrimac*'s guns dented the *Monitor*'s turret, but the vessel was not seriously damaged. Nor was the *Monitor* able to destroy the *Merrimac*. Their duel was a draw.

The battle was crucial, however, for it signaled the end of the era of wooden warships. Indeed, not long after the encounter, Gideon Welles ordered the construction of a number of shallow draft warships mounting two large guns for the Federal Navy, vessels that were especially designed for bombardment. These vessels were to be known as monitors.

The *Merrimac* was scuttled by its crew in May 1862 to prevent its capture by the Federals. The *Monitor* also came to an unfortunate end. Battered by a storm, the vessel sank in the waters off Cape Hatteras in December 1862. In 2002, divers managed to recover the *Monitor*'s rusted gun turret, its dents still visible. The ship's anchor, propeller, guns, and many of the ship's smaller artifacts have also been salvaged. Once conserved, many of these objects were put in exhibition at the Mariners' Museum in Newport News, Virginia.

Officers of the U.S.S. *Monitor* grouped by turret. James River, VA, July 9, 1862. James Gibson, photographer

Sailors of the U.S.S. *Monitor*, cookstove at left. James River, VA, July 9, 1862. James Gibson, photographer

Deck and turret of the U.S.S. *Monitor*. James River, VA, July 9, 1862. James Gibson, photographer

Captain W.N. Jeffers on the deck of the U.S.S. *Monitor*.
James River, VA, July 9, 1862. James Gibson, photographer

Sailors relaxing on the deck of the U.S.S. *Monitor*. James
River, VA, July 9, 1862. James Gibson, photographer

6 The Peninsular Campaign

Following the Federal debacle at Bull Run in July 1861, many Northern political and military leaders, as a way of easing their pain, conjured up a direct assault upon the Confederate capital of Richmond by the Army of the Potomac. Capturing Richmond, they reasoned, would not only wipe away the sour taste of the recent setback, it might even bring an end to the rebellion.

General George McClellan, who commanded the well-trained and powerful Army of the Potomac, agreed with this strategy. But McClellan opposed the accepted tactics, which called for following a route directly south to Richmond. McClellan had no wish to grapple with the Confederate forces under General Joseph E. Johnston in northern Virginia nor did he think well of the idea of having to negotiate the wide rivers that formed natural barriers between his army and the Confederate capital.

McClellan had a wholly different plan. He would move his army from Washington on a huge fleet of transports, steaming down the Potomac River into Chesapeake Bay and then directly south to Fort Monroe, a massive masonry fortification at the tip of the long peninsula formed by the York and James Rivers. From Fort Monroe, Richmond lay about one hundred miles to the north and west.

McClellan, however, was in no hurry to put his plan into action. He spent the waning months of 1861 and the rest of the winter drilling his troops and perfecting his strategy. Not until mid-March 1862 was the "Young Napoleon," as he was called, ready to move. ("Tardy George" was another of McClellan's nicknames, derived from his slowness in ordering his army into action.)

McClellan called upon vessels of every size and shape to relocate his army, more than 450 in all. In just three weeks, the Federals transported some 105,000 men, almost 15,000 horses and other animals, 1,200 wagons and ambulances, plus battery guns and other equipment to Fort Monroe. It was the largest movement of troops and supplies in American history up to that time.

Once settled at the tip of the peninsula, McClellan began a cautious advance. It was now early April. General Johnston had long since begun to shift his army out of northern Virginia toward Richmond. At Yorktown, in the path of McClellan's advance, Johnston had about 17,000 men under General John Magruder entrenched in earthworks left over from the Revolutionary War.

Although McClellan held a four-to-one advantage in troop strength over Magruder, the Union general believed he was greatly outnumbered. He thus decided his best strategy was to lay siege to Yorktown, a decision that gave Johnston even more time to shift his troops into position.

On May 3, Johnston abruptly abandoned Yorktown for a better defensive position that Confederate engineers had been preparing barely ten miles from Richmond. As they pulled back, the Confederates fought an all-day battle at Williamsburg, a delaying action meant to slow down McClellan's pursuing army.

On May 31, with Richmond at his back, Johnston attacked Union forces located between Fair Oaks Station and the town of Seven Pines. Had the assault been successful, it might have dealt McClellan's army a crippling blow. But Johnston wholly mismanaged the venture, which proved indecisive at best.

As he watched the battle unfold near Fair Oaks Station, Johnston was struck by a bullet in the shoulder and also by shell fragments in the chest. His recovery would take months.

Jefferson Davis named 55-year-old General Robert E. Lee, who had been serving as the Confederate president's military adviser, to take command of the Army of Northern Virginia. One of Lee's first moves was to dispatch a cavalry unit under General Jeb Stuart on a daring reconnaissance mission completely around the Federal army. Stuart and his men destroyed Union supplies, captured prisoners, and returned with news of weaknesses in McClellan's positions.

Lee also acted to bolster his army by summoning General Thomas J. "Stonewall" Jackson and his three divisions, about 18,500 men, from the Shenandoah Valley. There Jackson had conducted a brilliant campaign, swinging back and forth to win undisputed control of the Valley.

By the end of June, Lee was ready to set in motion a bold plan to blunt McClellan's advance. He marched some 55,000 men to the north bank of the Chickahominy River and launched a string of savage attacks against McClellan's exposed flank. They are known as the Seven Days' battles. They included Mechanicsville, Gaines' Mill, Savage Station, Frayser's Farm, and Malvern Hill. Federal artillery decimated the attacking Confederates, yet Lee's men managed to force McClellan's army back to Harrison's Landing on the banks of the James River. Richmond had been saved and the curtain had been rung down on McClellan's lofty peninsular campaign.

The photographs of the campaign are largely the work of James Gibson, a Scottish born cameraman who was several years younger than Brady. At the time, Gibson worked in the Brady studio in Washington, which was being managed by Alexander Gardner. John Wood, who is believed to have assisted Gibson, George Barnard, David Woodbury, and Gardner himself also covered the peninsular campaign.

Gibson was the most active of them all. He began his work early in May, photographing McClellan's headquarters, groups of officers, and Federal fortifications and encampments. When McClellan's army edged its way toward Richmond, Gibson went with them.

Some of the photographs that Gibson produced during this period are among the most dramatic of the war, sweeping views of men and their equipment and the quarters they occupied. These images are important if only because they give some understanding of the enormous size of McClellan's operation.

Gibson's work showed what could be accomplished by photographers in the field. "... we can assume that Gibson's colleagues were impressed by what he was able to produce at the front," writes William Frassanito in *Antietam: The Photographic Legacy of America's Bloodiest Day*. "Gibson proved it could be done, and others would soon follow his lead."

The photograph of the "Court House or City Hall" at Yorktown that appears in Chapter 1 (page 32) is of special interest. The figure standing at the left is believed by some to be Mathew Brady. The person's flat straw hat and long dark coat are articles of clothing that Brady favored.

Frassanito is one of those who questions whether the person is Brady. There is, he says, "an absence of evidence, photographic or otherwise, that he [Brady] accompanied his crew as this time . . . ."

Federal encampment. Cumberland Landing, va, May 1862. Photographer unidentified

Federal encampment on Pamunkey River. Cumberland Landing, va, May 1862. James Gibson, photographer

Federal supply vessels. White House Landing, VA, 1862. Photographer unidentified

Confederate fortifications with bales of cotton. Yorktown, VA, June 1862. Photographer unidentified

Federal artillery park. Yorktown, VA, May-August 1862.
Photographer unidentified

Camp Winfield Scott, Headquarters of General George
McClellan. Yorktown, VA, May 3, 1862. James Gibson,
photographer

Federal wagon park. Yorktown, VA, May – August 1862. Photographer unidentified

13-inch seacoast mortars of Federal Battery No. 4, with officers of 1st Connecticut Heavy Artillery. Yorktown, VA, vicinity, May 1862. James Gibson, photographer

Confederate water Battery Magruder, with Rodman smooth-bore siege guns. Yorktown, VA, June 1862. George Barnard, photographer

Embarkation for White House Landing. Yorktown, VA, May 1862. Photographer unidentified

Lt. James B. Washington, a Confederate prisoner, with Capt. George Custer. Fair Oaks, VA, May 31, 1862. James Gibson, photographer

Professor Thaddeus S. Lowe observing the battle from his balloon "Intrepid." Fair Oaks, VA, May 31, 1862. Photographer unidentified

Horatio Gibson's C and G Batteries. Fair Oaks, VA, vicinity, June 1862. James Gibson, photographer

Battery B, First New York Light Artillery.
Fair Oaks, VA, vicinity, June 1862.
George Barnard, photographer

Federal battery. Fair Oaks, VA, vicinity,
June 1862. Photographer unidentified

Twin Houses on battlefield, with 12-pounder field howitzer in foreground. Seven Pines, VA, June 1862. George Barnard, photographer

20-pounder Parrot guns of the 1st New York battery. Richmond, VA, vicinity, June 1862. James Gibson, photographer

Captured Confederate howitzer near Hanover Courthouse. The Peninsula, VA, May – August 1862. Photographer unidentified

Grapevine bridge built by the 5th New Hampshire Infantry. Chickahominy River, VA, May – August 1862. David Woodbury, photographer

Group of "contrabands" at
Foller's house. Cumberland
Landing, VA, May 14, 1862.
James Gibson, photographer

Engineers building corduroy road. Cumberland Landing, VA,
June 1862. David Woodbury, photographer

Headquarters of General McClellan. Savage Station, VA, June 27, 1862. George Barnard, photographer

Field hospital after battle of June 27. Savage Station, VA, June 30, 1862. James Gibson, photographer

Members of class of 1860, U.S. Military Academy.
Harrison's Landing, VA, July 1862.
Alexander Gardner, photographer

Group of the Irish Brigade. Harrison's Landing, VA,
July 1862. Photographer unidentified

Confederate battery Magruder with 8-inch
Columbiads. Yorktown, VA, June 1862.
Photographer unidentified

Ruins of Gaines' Mill. Cold Harbor, VA, April 1865.
John Reekie, photographer

White Oak Swamp. White Oak
Swamp, VA, May-August 1862.
Photographer unidentified

7 The Second Battle of Bull Run (Manassas)

Late in July 1862, with General Lee still occupied by General McClellan's huge Army of the Potomac that was concentrated south and east of Richmond, another Federal force, under General John Pope, left Washington and marched south through Manassas to threaten the Confederate capital from the north. Lee reacted by sending Stonewall Jackson from Richmond to counter Pope's move. At the same time, Lee kept an eye on McClellan.

On August 9, Jackson's army of 24,000 collided with some 9,000 men under Major General Nathaniel Banks at Cedar Mountain in Virginia, near Culpeper. Banks launched a spirited assault but was repelled by a crushing counterattack led by General A. P. Hill, a veteran of the Mexican War.

By this time, Lee knew that McClellan had been ordered to abandon his peninsular campaign and shift some of his troop strength to reinforce Pope. Lee quickly joined Jackson against Pope.

Jackson's "foot cavalry" then made one of the war's most notable marches. Concealed behind a mountain range, Jackson's men trekked fifty miles around Pope's flank to destroy the Federal supply depot at Manassas Junction. Pope turned back and initiated a series of attacks against Jackson that led to the Second Battle of Bull Run.

On August 29, the battle's first day, Pope launched a series of piecemeal attacks against Jackson's position, all of which were repulsed. Both sides suffered heavy casualties. Pope attacked again, unaware that Confederate General James Longstreet and his troops had arrived to reinforce Jackson. The battle's climax came when Longstreet counterattacked in what was the largest mass assault of the war up to that time. Longstreet punished Pope's left flank and drove his army back toward the fortifications of Washington.

For the second time in little more than a year, the Federals had been defeated at Bull Run. More important, practically all of Virginia was now in the hands of Lee and the Confederates.

Cedar Mountain, VA. Battlefield viewed from the west, August 1862. Timothy O'Sullivan, photographer

Cedar Mountain, VA. Federal battery fording a tributary of the Rappahannock River, August 1862. Timothy O'Sullivan, photographer

Fauquier Sulphur Springs, VA. Federal troops building bridges across the north fork of the Rappahannock River, August 1862. Timothy O'Sullivan, photographer

Rappahannock River, VA.
Bridge over the Rappahannock
River, August 1862. Timothy
O'Sullivan, photographer

Manassas, VA. Co. C, 41st New
York Infantry, July 1862.
Timothy O'Sullivan,
photographer

Manassas Junction, VA. Federal soldiers beside
damaged stock of Orange & Alexandria Railroad,
August 1862. Timothy O'Sullivan, photographer.

Rappahannock River, VA. Fugitive African-Americans
fording the Rappahannock River, August 1862.
Timothy O'Sullivan, photographer

8 Army Life

When the Civil War became a reality, most Northerners and Southerners greeted the news enthusiastically, and thousands rushed to enlist with a sense of excitement and adventure. So great was the flood of recruits that government manpower quotas were quickly surpassed. But the new enlistees were quickly jolted out of their exuberance when they arrived at camp to find themselves lodged in two-by-four tents or hastily built wooden shelters. To go along with inadequate quarters, recruits were made to cope with slipshod training, shoddy equipment, poor food, and medical treatment suited for the Dark Ages.

At the beginning, military discipline in Federal camps was generally lacking, at least in part because most young recruits had a stubborn and independent nature born of the democratic freedoms they had come to enjoy. The fact that there were few officer-candidate schools in the North or South to train prospective leaders worsened the problem. Any Federal regiment headed by a colonel who was a West Point graduate was considered very fortunate. As the war dragged on, the situation improved. Soldiers would say, "Yes, sir," and salute, but discipline seldom approached the standards of the European military tradition.

Training included a steady diet of drilling and marching. Recruits were taught how to stand at attention, how to shoulder a rifle, and "Right face!" "Left face!" "Present arms!" and all the rest.

Recruits complained about having to drill and march so much. All the training was meant to teach troops how to shift from a formation on the march into a unit that was ready to fight. On a country road, a regiment (10 companies, or 1,000 men) might march in a column of fours. When the formation reached the battle site, it changed. Instead of arranging themselves in columns, troops usually drew up abreast, elbow to elbow, to form a battle line or several lines. Once fighting began, the line might be ordered to shift to the right or left or to advance or retreat. Drilling was meant to prepare troops to perform these and other tactical maneuvers.

While drilling was almost constant, training with rifles was another matter. A high proportion of recruits had never fired a rifle. Nevertheless, rifle practice was a rarity. After the battle of Gettysburg in July 1863, ordnance officers recovered thousands of rifles that had been loaded and even reloaded—without ever being fired.

In camp, diseases such as dysentery and pneumonia, and such "camp fevers" as typhoid, typhus, and malaria were rampant. The medical establishment of the day did not know what caused these diseases; they had no idea how to treat them. An estimated 620,000 military men died during the Civil War, according to *The Library of Congress Civil War Desk Reference*. Twice as many died of disease than died in battle.

Soldiers unfortunate enough to have to sleep in tents and be exposed to cold, snow, and rain were more susceptible to disease than those assigned to barracks. Often six men slept in a tent designed for four. The smaller two-man tent was so modest in size that it was said to be more suitable for a dog, a small dog at that. The tent became known as a "dog shanty" or "pup tent."

Barracks, normally overcrowded, were scarcely better. Men were vulnerable to contagious diseases, or what was called "crowd poisoning."

Civil War soldiers encamped in one place usually received an adequate amount of food. Salt pork was the chief meat source. A large cracker, known as hardtack, served as bread. Beans or peas were the vegetables. Fresh green vegetables were practically unknown.

Early in the war, troops took turns cooking. Frying was the standard method of preparing food. In 1863, the U.S. Congress mandated the use of company cooks. Both Union and Confederate armies often detailed African-Americans to do this work.

When not drilling or performing guard duty, there was little for soldiers to do in most camps. Reading and letter writing were the chief means of overcoming boredom. When paper was in short supply, men would reuse letters they had received by writing between the lines. Postage was cheap and postal systems generally efficient. Cards and checkers were popular, too. So were gambling and drinking, although both were unsanctioned activities.

Despite disease, boredom, loneliness, the many uncertainties, the horror of battle, with the possibility of death or disabling injury, many thousands of men on both sides of the conflict maintained their courage and determination right to the war's end. More than a few historians consider Civil War soldiers to be among the best fighting men of all time.

Infantry private. Unknown location, 1861. Photographer unidentified

B-88

Infantry camp. Unknown location,
1861–1865. Photographer unidentified

Camp of 50th New York Engineers.
Rappahannock Station, VA, March 1864.
Photographer unknown

Company G, 93rd New York Infantry. Bealeton, VA, August 1863. Timothy O'Sullivan, photographer

Federal encampment. Cumberland Landing, VA, May 1862. Photographer unknown

Army of the Potomac Head-
quarters. Brandy Station, VA,
April 1864. Photographer
unknown

Infantry company resting
from drills. Unknown location,
1861–1865. Photographer
unidentified

Camp of 18th Pennsylvania Cavalry.
Unknown location, 1861.
Photographer unidentified

Quarters of Capt. Harry Clinton,
Quartermaster, Provost Marshal
Dept. Brandy Station, VA, 1864.
Photographer unidentified

26th New York Infantry on parade. Fort Lyon, VA, 1861–1865. Photographer unidentified

Infantry company assembled for parade. Unknown location, 1861–1865. Photographer unidentified

Infantry company on parade. Unknown location, 1861–1865. Photographer unidentified

Soldiers' "pine cottage" winter quarters. Unknown location, 1861–1865. Photographer unidentified

Regimental parade. Unknown
location, 1861–1865.
Photographer unidentified

Infantry company at "parade
rest". Unknown location,
1861–1865. Photographer
unidentified

Commissary Depot. Cedar Level,
VA, 1861–1865. Photographer
unidentified

Regimental drum corps. Unknown
location, 1861–1865. Photographer
unidentified

Noncommissioned officers' mess, Co. D., 93rd Infantry. Bealeton, VA, August 1863. Photographer unidentified

Federal camp by the Tennessee River. Chattanooga, TN, Vicinity, ca. 1864. Photographer unidentified

9 Antietam

Early in September 1862, General Lee marched his army across the Potomac River and into Maryland in what was his first invasion of the North. Lee believed that he had good reasons for doing so. He hoped to encourage the people of Maryland, a border state, to swing to the side of the Confederacy. Just as important, Lee thought that if his invasion could be successful it might induce the British and perhaps also the French to grant recognition to the Confederacy. Much needed foreign aid might then follow.

As he moved into Maryland, Lee divided his army, assigning Jackson and his men to capture Harper's Ferry, while Longstreet and his divisions were ordered to advance toward Hagerstown.

McClellan, meanwhile, headed northwest out of Washington and toward Frederick, Maryland. He moved slowly, unsure of Lee's intent. During the march, McClellan enjoyed a stroke of good fortune. A corporal from an Indiana regiment happened to find a bundle of three cigars lying in the grass near his camp. The cigars were wrapped in a copy of Lee's actual battle plan, which was quickly transmitted to McClellan.

Now aware of Confederate tactics, McClellan ordered his army to march westward to take advantage of Lee's divided force. But McClellan failed to move fast enough and his caution made it possible for Lee to reunite his scattered army. By September 16, Lee had some 40,000 troops on the hills above Antietam Creek near the village of Sharpsburg, Maryland. On the other side of the creek, McClellan had approximately 75,000 men who were preparing for battle.

The next day, September 17, savage fighting began at dawn and continued through the day and into the night. Instead of using his superior force in an all out assault upon the thin Confederate line, McClellan sent his troops into action in a series of separate attacks. Lee, meanwhile, shifted his men back and forth in a desperate attempt to hold the line. Fighting engulfed the Dunker Church, Sunken Road, Miller's Cornfield, and places that were to become known as Bloody Lane and Burnside's Bridge.

Late in the afternoon, a Federal onslaught came close to overwhelming the Confederate rear and cutting off any path of escape. But the timely arrival of General A. P. Hill with 23,000 fresh reinforcements from Harper's Ferry helped to save the day.

Darkness ended the fighting. Of the 115,000 men that fought that day, 22,000 were killed or wounded. It still stands as the bloodiest day in American history.

The next day was relatively quiet, with only minor skirmishes. Lee's army was exhausted, badly mangled and, as he realized, heavily outnumbered. He elected to end his Maryland campaign. During the night and through the next day, Lee led his weary men back across the Potomac and into the Shenandoah Valley.

Hardly had the guns fallen silent at Antietam when Alexander Gardner and James Gibson arrived on the scene. The pair made nearly one hundred photographs of the region and notable battlefield landmarks. Gardner's first photograph, depicting dead solders near Dunker Church, is dated September 19, the date of Lee's withdrawal. He and Gibson worked for three more days, according to research conducted by William Frassanito. Gardner returned to Antietam early in October to document Abraham Lincoln's visit to the battle site.

Both Gardner and Gibson were employed by Mathew Brady at the time. So it was late in October in 1862 that Brady displayed many of their Antietam photographs at his gallery in New York City. "At the door of his [Brady's] gallery hangs a little placard 'The Dead of Antietam,'" *The New York Times* noted, and observed, " … crowds of people are constantly going up the stairs."

The Times declared, "Mr. Brady has done something to bring home to us the terrible reality and earnestness of war. If he has not brought bodies and laid them in our dooryards and along streets, he has done something very like it."

In the *Atlantic Monthly*, Oliver Wendell Holmes wrote, "Let him who wants to know what war is, look at these series of illustrations." Holmes' son, a Union captain, was badly wounded at Antietam.

In the months that followed, the photographs were offered as small album photos, and as stereographs. The photographs of human bodies proved especially popular in these formats.

The Antietam photographs by Gardner, O'Sullivan, and Gibson set the course for battlefield photography through much of the rest of the war, as William Frassanito has pointed out. War photographers would concentrate on battlefield carnage whenever possible.

Antietam Bridge on the Sharpsburg-Boonsboro Turnpike. Antietam, MD, September 1862. Alexander Gardner, photographer

Burnside's bridge. Antietam, MD, September 1862.
Alexander Gardner, photographer

Signal tower overlooking Antietam battlefield.
Elk Mountain, MD, September 1862. Timothy
O'Sullivan, photographer

Confederate soldiers as they fell near the Burnside bridge. Antietam, MD, September 1862. Alexander Gardner, photographer

Bodies of Confederate dead gathered for burial.
Antietam, MD, September 1862. Alexander Gardner,
photographer

Lutheran Church. Sharpsburg, MD, September 1862.
Alexander Gardner, photographer

Ruins of arsenal. Harper's Ferry, wv, October 1862. David Woodbury

Confederate wounded at Smith's barn. Keedysville, md, September 1862. Alexander Gardner, photographer

Bodies in front of Dunker church. Antietam, MD, September 1862. Photographer unidentified

Confederate dead by a fence on the Hagerstown Road. Antietam, MD, September 1862. Alexander Gardner, photographer

Allan Pinkerton of the Secret Service. Antietam, MD, September 1862. Alexander Gardner, photographer

Allan Pinkerton, President Lincoln, and Major General John A. McClernand. Antietam, MD, October 3, 1862. Alexander Gardner, photographer

President Lincoln and General McClellan in the general's tent. Antietam, MD, October 3, 1862. Alexander Gardner, photographer

President Lincoln with General McClellan and group of officers. Antietam, MD, October 3, 1862. Alexander Gardner, photographer

Pontoon bridge and ruins of stone bridge. Berlin (now Brunswick), MD, September 1862. Alexander Gardner, photographer

Ruins of railroad bridge. Harper's Ferry, WV, September-October 1862. C. O. Bostwick, photographer

10 Fredericksburg and Chancellorsville

As General Lee led his badly crippled army across the Potomac and into Virginia following the fierce fighting at Antietam, McClellan made no great effort to pursue him. For this inaction, McClellan was sharply criticized by Northern newspapers. And his failure to follow-up what had been, strategically, at least, a Northern victory, was a deciding factor in Lincoln's decision to strip McClellan of his command.

In November 1862, Lincoln appointed General Ambrose Burnside head of the Army of the Potomac. Burnside was regarded as being a more aggressive leader than his predecessor.

Burnside secured Lincoln's approval for a new campaign against Richmond, a piece of planning that led to the general's forces being crushed at Fredericksburg in December 1862 in what was one of the Union's worst defeats of the war. Casualties on both sides totaled 18,000; two-thirds of the men killed, wounded, or missing were Federal.

After Burnside's bloody defeat at Fredericksburg, General Joseph—"Fighting Joe"—Hooker was named by Lincoln to supplant him as commander of the Army of the Potomac. Late in April 1863, Hooker attempted to outflank the well-entrenched Confederate army at Fredericksburg. All went well at first. But Lee reacted by dividing his smaller force and defeating Hooker at the battle of Chancellorsville. The Confederate army performed so brilliantly there that Chancellorsville has become known as "Lee's masterpiece." Although a stunning victory for Lee, the South had to bear the loss of Stonewall Jackson, mortally wounded by the accidental fire of his own soldiers.

Since Fredericksburg and Chancellorsville were both Northern defeats, the most active cameramen of the time had no opportunity to visit the battle sites. The views presented here were taken in the general area of the two towns before the fighting began or after the guns had fallen silent.

His victory at Chancellorsville gave Lee momentum. Early in the summer of 1863, he crossed the Potomac once more and headed north into Pennsylvania.

The town from the east bank of the Rappahonnock River. Fredricksburg, VA, March 1863. Timothy O'Sullivan, photographer

Federal supply depot. Aquia Creek Landing, VA, February 1863. Alexander Gardner, photographer

Wharf with transport vessel and supplies. Aquia Creek Landing, VA, November 1862-April 1863. Photographer unidentified

Personnel in front of quartermaster's office. Aquia Creek Landing, VA, February 1863. Alexander Gardner, photographer

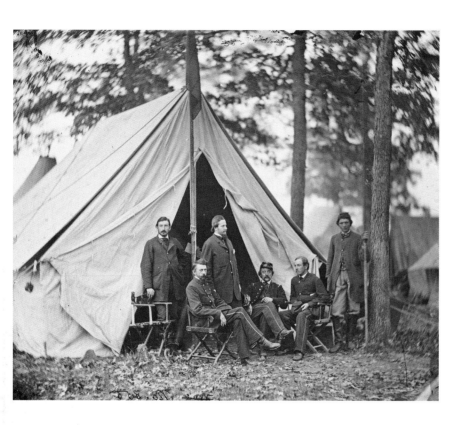

Dr. Jonathan Letterman, medical director of the Army of the Potomac, and his staff. Warrenton, VA, November 1862. Photographer unidentified

General Ambrose Burnside and his staff. Warrenton, VA, November 1862. Photographer unidentified

Captain George Custer and General
Alfred Pleasonton. Falmouth, VA, April 1863.
Timothy Sullivan, photographer

Army of Potomac headquarters, group in front of Post Office. Falmouth, VA, April 1863. Timothy Sullivan, photographer

Drum Corps of the 61st New York Infantry. Falmouth, VA, March 1863. Timothy Sullivan, photographer

11 Gettysburg

By the end of June 1863, General Lee's army was well into Pennsylvania, his men subsisting on what they could forage from the bountiful farms of Northerners. One column of his troops loomed as a threat to Harrisburg, coming within a few miles of the state capital. Another detachment veered toward York on the Susquehanna River.

Lee had freedom of movement because the Army of the Potomac, commanded by General Joseph Hooker, was still south of the Potomac River. But then Lee learned that the Federal columns had crossed the Potomac and were converging on Frederick, Maryland. Lee was also brought the news that Hooker was no longer in command of the Army of the Potomac. Lincoln had replaced him with the very competent General George G. Meade, a Pennsylvanian.

Lee's response was to order his wide-roaming columns to end their wandering and gather at Gettysburg, a quiet Pennsylvania crossroads, its landscape dominated by ridges and hills. Meade also issued orders directing his army to converge at Gettysburg. The two armies were now on a collision course, Lee marching in from the north, Meade moving up from the south.

Shortly after dawn on July 1, the fighting began. The Federals, badly outnumbered at the time, offered only a delaying action until the rest of the army arrived. Lee's men steadily pushed the Northerners back through the town. The Federals, nevertheless, managed to hold the high ground on Gettysburg's northern and eastern slopes.

That night reinforcements arrived. Now Meade had the advantage.

The next day Lee attacked, striking the Federal left flank at the Peach Orchard, the Wheatfield, Devil's Den, and Big and Little Round Tops, and later pressing the other flank at Culp's Hill and Cemetery Hill. The Federals, with the advantage of high ground and potent artillery, withstood every attack.

On July 3, Lee made the decision to make one more assault on the Federal lines. He amassed 12,000 Confederate infantrymen for the attack. At mid-afternoon, following a long artillery bombardment, the Southerners launched a frontal charge across a mile of open ground aimed at the center of the Federal position. Although mauled by both long- and short-range fire, Pickett's Charge, as it was called—named for General George E. Pickett, one of its commanders—managed to pierce the Federal line momentarily, but ultimately was driven back.

"The Southerners had won the first two days of the battle but lost the third." Lee called for a retreat. Once again he had failed in his quest for a victory in the North.

Gettysburg was the biggest battle of the Civil War. Both sides sustained enormous losses. The Confederates suffered 28,000 casualties, a third of the entire army. Lee also lost seventeen of fifty-two generals. The Federals had 23,000 casualties.

As Lee retreated, the North rejoiced. "The chain of Robert Lee's invincibility is broken," wrote diarist George Templeton Strong. "The Army of the Potomac has at last found a general that can handle it, and has stood nobly up to its terrible work in spite of its long disheartening list of hard-fought failures . . . ."

Then came more good news for the North. On July 4, Confederate General John C. Pemberton surrendered to Grant at Vicksburg. The two victories were a turning point in the war. Northerners now believed they were on the track to final victory.

Alexander Gardner and the two cameramen from his Washington studio, Timothy O'Sullivan and James Gibson, were the first photographers to arrive at Gettysburg following the battle. Traveling as a team, the three took their first photographs not long after Lee had withdrawn from the battlefield, late in the morning on July 5, 1863, according to William Frassanito in *Gettysburg: A Journey in Time*, his meticulous study of the Gettysburg photographs.

"It is by no means an overstatement," writes Frassanito, "that Gardner's prime concern was to record the horrors of war rather than the area's landmarks or general views of the terrain." About three-quarters of Gardner's sixty or so photographs depict swollen corpses, open graves, dead horses, and other such subjects relating to Gettysburg's terrible slaughter. There was a commercial reason for this. Such scenes were snapped up quickly by the general public.

Mathew Brady and his assistants arrived at Gettysburg on or about July 15, well after the Gardner team had departed. Brady, traveling from New York, had a much longer journey than Gardner, Gettysburg being only about seventy-five miles from Washington. Brady may possibly have been delayed by the turmoil in New York. Efforts to enforce the first Federal conscription act had enraged the city's Irish workers. In June 1863, Federal troops had to be summoned to protect black strikebreakers during a strike by Irish longshoreman. Hostility toward President Lincoln and black laborers ultimately resulted in the draft riots of mid-July, which have been cited as the bloodiest urban disturbance in American history. Perhaps Brady looked upon his trek to Gettysburg as a welcome relief from the chaos of New York.

By the time Brady arrived at the site, the battlefield had been cleared of bodies. Brady and his assistants took about thirty photographs, concentrating on panoramic views and landmarks that had come into prominence during the three-day struggle. Photographs that depict Brady himself were also made, taken no doubt to document his presence at the battle site.

Alfred Waud, artist for *Harper's Weekly*, sketching
on battlefield. Gettysburg, PA, July 1863. Timothy
O'Sullivan, photographer

Headquarters of General Robert
E. Lee. Gettysburg, PA, July 1863.
Brady studio

Six officers of the 17th New York
battery. Gettysburg, PA, June 1863.
Photographer unidentified

Breastworks on the left wing of the Federal line. Gettysburg, PA, July 1863. Brady studio

Interior view of breastworks on extreme left of the Federal line. Gettysburg, PA, July 1863. Alexander Gardner, photographer

Center of the Federal position viewed from Little Round Top. Gettysburg, PA, July 1863. Alexander Gardner, photographer

Bodies of Federal soldiers killed near the McPherson woods. Gettysburg, PA, July 1863. Timothy O'Sullivan, photographer

391

Battered trees on Culp's hill.
Gettysburg, PA, 1863.
Photographer unidentified

Confederate prisoners.
Gettysburg, PA, July 1863.
Brady studio

Dead soldiers in the woods near Little Round Top. Gettysburg, PA, July 1863. Alexander Gardner, photographer

Devil's Den with dead Confederate soldier. Gettysburg, PA, July 1863. Alexander Gardner, photographer

Confederate soldiers slain on Round Top.
Gettysburg, PA, July 1863. Photographer unidentified

Cemetery Gatehouse. Gettysburg, PA, July 1863.
Brady studio

12 Winter Quarters at Brandy Station

Following the battle of Gettysburg until the end of 1863, General Meade's Army of the Potomac maneuvered about with little effect. Hope for success in a lively skirmish at Mine Run, Virginia, west of Fredericksburg, was subverted by bad weather and excess caution on the part of one of Meade's field commanders. The failure to move quickly and decisively allowed Lee to establish strong field fortifications on the west bank of Mine Run, just south of a densely forested area known as the Wilderness, where General Hooker had been vanquished at Chancellorsville just a year before.

Rather than confront the well-fortified Lee, Meade withdrew north to Brandy Station, Virginia, between the Rappahonnock and Rapidan Rivers, and there established winter quarters for his men. Across the Rapidan, less than

thirty miles southwest of Brandy Station, near the village of Orange, General Lee set up a winter place of lodging for his Army of Northern Virginia.

After more than two years of fighting, the Civil War was at a standstill. But some of the most ferocious and bloody fighting lay just ahead.

In March 1864, President Lincoln made a decision that would have far-reaching results. He called General Grant to Washington and in a well-deserved promotion made him general of all the Federal armies.

Straightforward and strong-willed, Grant believed the military problem to be quite simple. The Confederate armies had to be destroyed. It was his contention that Federal armies had been pursuing the war "like a balky team, no two pulling together." Grant's plan was to strike simultaneously in all theaters of operation. Lee would be unable to shift his outnumbered forces to meet the coordinated attacks. Grant wanted total war.

In a change in policy, Grant announced that he would not command Federal forces from Washington, as had his predecessors. He would establish his headquarters with General Meade's Army of the Potomac, coordinating the movement of Federal troops in the East by telegraph. To head Federal operations in the West, Grant chose his close and trusted friend and outstanding field commander General William T. Sherman.

In accord with the strategy outlined by Grant, Meade's army was to press down upon Richmond from the north. At the same time, General Benjamin Butler's Army of the James would move toward the Confederate capital out of the southeast along the James River. General Franz Sigel and a third column of Federal troops were to open operations in the Shenandoah Valley, destroying Lee's food sources.

The months in winter quarters were a time of relative calm for the soldiers of both armies. While there were drills, inspections, and picket duty, when men were assigned to forward positions to warn of an enemy presence, there was also time for letter writing, reading newspapers, visiting friends in seldom seen units, and welcoming visitors, even occasionally women.

For photographers, winter quarters was a profitable time. Local photographers set up small field studios to make likenesses of individual soldiers. These were reproduced as *cartes de visite* or tintypes to be mailed back home.

For experienced field photographers such as Timothy O'Sullivan (many of whose photographs are offered in this section), the slackening of activity during the weeks at winter quarters was a period of great opportunity. Because of the camera's technical limitations, photography of the day had to be devoted to static studies. What could be better than having the army at rest? Soldiers could be gathered together and posed in group photographs. Zouaves in the unconventional uniforms appear frequently for such pictures. Winter quarters photographs also depicted places of shelter and encampment and the different types of equipment that various units used.

By the first week of May, Grant was ready to roll. On May 2, 1864, the various corps, division, brigade, and regimental commanders of the Army of the Potomac received operational orders. The first sentence read: "The army will move on Wednesday, the 4th of May, 1864." This terse statement signaled the beginning of operations that would be among the bloodiest in American history, causing even Northerners to refer to Grant as "a butcher."

Canvas pontoon boat, 50th New York Engineers. Rappahannock Station, VA, March 1864. Timothy H. O'Sullivan, photographer

Scouts and guides of the Army of the Potomac. Brandy Station, VA, March 1864. Photographer unidentified

Headquarters, 1st Brigade, Horse Artillery. Brandy Station, VA, February 1864. Photographer unidentified

Wagon park. Brandy Station, VA, May 1864.
Timothy O'Sullivan, photographer

Band of the 114th Pennsylvania Infantry (Zouaves).
Brandy Station, VA, April 1864. Timothy O'Sullivan,
photographer

Guard mount of the 114th Pennsylvania Infantry
Division, 1st Division, 3rd Corps. Brandy Station, VA,
March 1864. Timothy O'Sullivan, photographer

General Rufus Ingalls. Brandy Station, VA, April 1864.
Timothy O'Sullivan, photographer

Headquarters, winter quarters, Army of the
Potomac. Brandy Station, VA, February 1864.
Photographer unidentified

Dinner party, Army of Potomac Headquarters.
Brandy Station, VA, April 1864.
Timothy O'Sullivan, photographer

13 Grant's Wilderness Campaign, Spotsylvania, Cold Harbor

On May 4, 1864, as Grant had ordered, the Army of the Potomac, now numbering 120,000 men, headed south out of Brandy Station and crossed the Rapidan River. Timothy O'Sullivan, working for Alexander Gardner at the time, went with the troops. "It is almost certain," writes William Frassanito, "that O'Sullivan, a civilian, was the only photographer (together with his assistants) who was with the army at this time."

Grant's strategy was to push quickly southward, slipping through the heavily forested Wilderness area to advance into open country beyond Lee's flank. But Lee discovered what Grant was trying to do and blocked his advance. The Battle of the Wilderness was the result. The tangled undergrowth prevented use of wheeled vehicles, making it an infantryman's struggle, with infantrymen charging and countercharging through the dark woods for two days.

Lee managed to stop Grant but only temporarily. Grant moved forward again, attempting to position his army between Lee and Richmond. Again Lee checked Grant's movement, this time at Spotsylvania, a few miles south of the Wilderness. Another horrific battle ensued, lasting for two weeks. The worst fighting took place on May 12, when an early morning Federal attack forced a V-shaped breach in the Confederate line. In rain and mud, the Confederates counterattacked and barely managed to hold their position.

An awesome number of men were killed or wounded during the struggles at the Wilderness and Spotsylvania. The Federals came away with some 35,000 casualties in just two weeks of fighting. The Confederates suffered 17,000 casualties, a number that was proportionately almost as high.

Despite the losses, Grant remained determined. "I will take no backward steps," he said. "I propose to fight it out on this line if it takes all summer." For several days, the two armies sparred with one another as Grant continued in his effort to turn Lee's right flank and get behind his lines. More bloody fighting took place along the North Anna River.

On June 2, the two armies came face to face once more in the vicinity of Cold Harbor, a vital crossroads about ten miles northeast of Richmond. Here Grant would make what would be judged as one of his biggest mistakes of the war. At dawn on June 3, he ordered a frontal assault. More than 40,000 of Grant's men surged forward along a mile-and-a-half front to attack an enemy entrenched in an elaborate network of earthworks. Outright slaughter was the result. By noon, some 7,000 Federals were killed or wounded and had gained no particular advantage.

By now, the armies of the North and South had been involved in almost ceaseless fighting for almost a month. Both sides had suffered great losses. But whereas Grant replaced the killed and wounded within a matter of weeks, Lee was never able to restore his front-line forces to their regular fighting strength.

Timothy O'Sullivan continued his coverage of Grant's campaign into the early weeks of June. By then, Mathew Brady himself and a number of his cameramen were present at Cold Harbor. They did not record any battlefield views. They instead turned up at Grant's headquarters behind the lines, and there concentrated on making portraits of Grant, his generals, and members of their staffs. A full-length portrait of a frowning Grant leaning against a small and spindly pine tree has been described by Salon.com as a "cranky, get-it-over-with photograph" that would prove to be "Brady's masterpiece . . ."

Soldiers filling canteens. Fredericksburg, VA,
May 1864. Photographer unidentified

Field telegraph station. Wilcox's Landing, VA,
vicinity, May 1864. Photographer unidentified

2507

Wounded from the Battle of the Wilderness. Fredericksburg, VA, May 1864. James Gardner, photographer

Burial of soldiers. Fredericksburg, VA, May 1864. Timothy O'Sullivan, photographer

50th New York Engineers building a road along the
south bank of the North Anna River. Jericho Mills, VA,
May 24, 1864. Timothy O'Sullivan, photographer

Canvas pontoon bridge across the North Anna River.
Jericho Mills, VA, May 24, 1864. Timothy O'Sullivan,
photographer

Destroyed bridge of the Richmond and Fredericksburg Railroad. North Anna River, VA, May 25, 1864. Timothy O'Sullivan, photographer

Federal troops occupying line of breastworks on north bank of North Anna River. May 1864. Timothy O'Sullivan

Rappahannock River front during Grant's withdrawal. Port Royal, VA, May 30, 1864. Timothy O'Sullivan, photographer

Transports being loaded during Grant's withdrawal. Port Royal, VA, May 30, 1864. Timothy O'Sullivan, photographer

General Grant (left end of bench nearest tree) writing a dispatch. Massaponax Church, VA, May 21, 1864. Timothy O'Sullivan, photographer

General Grant, General Meade, Assistant Secretary of War Charles Dana, and staff officers. Massaponax Church, VA, May 21, 1864. Timothy O'Sullivan, photographer

Body of a Confederate soldier. Spotsylvania Court House, VA, May 1864.
Timothy O'Sullivan, photographer

Body of a Confederate soldier. Spotsylvania Court House, VA, May 1864.
Timothy O'Sullivan, photographer

B-12

230

General Grant and staff. Cold
Harbor, VA, June 11 or 12, 1864.
Mathew Brady studio

General Grant and staff. Cold
Harbor, VA, June 11 or 12, 1864.
Mathew Brady studio

African-Americans collecting the bones and remains of soldiers killed in battle. Cold Harbor, VA, April 1865. John Reekie, photographer

Photographer's wagon and tent. Cold Harbor, VA, May–June 1864. Unidentified photographer

447

14 The Army of the James

Early in May 1864, as Grant brawled with Lee's Army of Virginia in the Wilderness, General Benjamin Butler's 39,000 Federals that made up the Army of the James crossed the James River to land at Bermuda Hundred, a neck of land of about fifteen miles south of Richmond. Butler made an uninspired strike toward the city, then called for a pause in his operation.

General P. G. T. Beauregard, leading a Confederate force from Petersburg, arrived to give Butler's army a drubbing at Drewy's Bluff, and later managed to seal up the Federal general and his troops behind their own defenses that had been laid across the neck of the Bermuda Hundred peninsula. The Army of the James, said Grant, is "as completely shut off from further operations against Richmond as if it had been a bottle strongly corked." With Butler's

threat to Richmond ended, General Lee was able to send reinforcements from Bermuda Hundred to aid in the defense of Richmond.

During the summer of 1864, Butler hatched an idea that would permit Federal gunboats to travel up the James River. At the time, shelling from Confederate artillery batteries at Trent's Reach prevented the passage of such vessels. Butler's plan, approved by Grant, involved digging a shortcut across Dutch Gap, a stretch of land less than 200 miles in width.

Work on the project began on August 10, 1864. At times, as many as 1,500 men labored with shovels and picks. By December 31, 1864, construction was at its final stage. The explosion of a 12,000-pound powder charge was supposed to rip open the last remaining barrier, and water was expected to start flowing through the channel. Unfortunately, much of the exploded debris fell back into the cut, and the waterway remained securely blocked.

What happened at the Dutch Gap was one more in a long list of "Bottled up" Butler's fiascos. Grant, with Lincoln's approval, was to relieve him of his command early in 1865.

African-American soldiers at rest. Aiken's Landing, VA,
c. November 1864. Photographer unidentified

Confederate gun emplacement at Trent's Reach.
James River, VA, April 1865. Photographer unidentified

Photographer's wagon at General Butler's signal tower. Bermuda Hundred, VA, 1864. Photographer unidentified

African-American teamsters. Bermuda Hundred, VA, 1864. Photographer unidentified

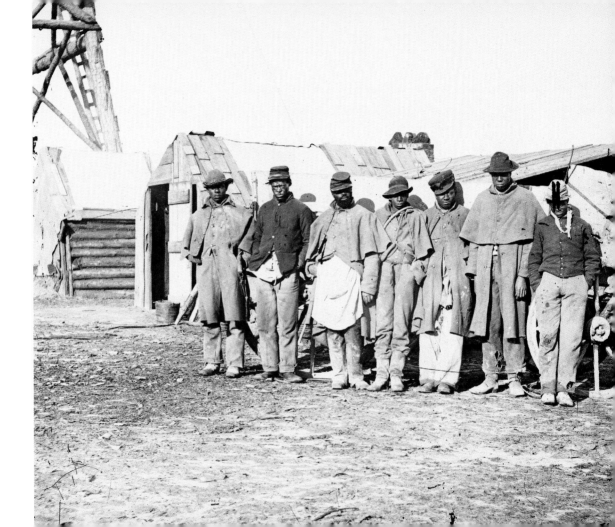

499

Officers of 1st Connecticut
Artillery. Fort Brady, VA, 1864.
Photographer unidentified

Dutch Gap Canal under construction. Dutch Gap, VA, November 1864. Photographer unidentified

Completed Dutch Gap canal. Dutch Gap, VA, November 1864. Photographer unidentified

15 The Siege of Petersburg

After his costly assault at Cold Harbor, Grant realized that a direct attack upon Richmond was out of the question. He had one final move. Twenty-two miles south of the Confederate capital lay Petersburg, a railroad junction that linked Richmond to the South. Early in June, Grant made a decision secretly to withdraw from Cold Harbor, cross the James River, subdue Petersburg, and then strike north.

On the night of June 12, 1864, Grant's troops quietly abandoned their entrenched positions at Cold Harbor to march south toward the James. The move was executed so skillfully that for hours Lee did not know the whereabouts of Grant's army. At Weyanoke Point on the James, Grant's engineers assembled a huge pontoon bridge. Troops were also ferried across the river.

Petersburg was only lightly defended when Grant's advance units began to arrive, but early attacks by the Army of the Potomac were tentative and poorly coordinated. An opportunity to take Petersburg was allowed to slip away.

By June 16, General Meade had the Army of the Potomac in position and ordered a frontal assault on Confederate lines. General Beauregard brought in every man he could find to hold off the attackers. After bitter fighting, Beauregard moved his army to a more secure line of entrenchments closer to Petersburg. Then heavy reinforcements arrived from General Lee.

On June 18, Meade saw that the situation had become hopeless and called off the attack. Once again, the armies of Lee and Grant were face to face.

Grant began to make preparations for a siege. His engineers constructed an intricate mix of forts, artillery positions, and entrenchments. The siege was to last ten months.

Grant set up his headquarters several miles northeast of Petersburg at City Point, Virginia, on a steep-faced hill formed by the meeting of the James and Appomattox Rivers. There an enormous supply base was established, similar in concept to Cam Ranh Bay during the war in Vietnam. Ships brought in tons of arms and provisions daily, which were to be hauled to the troops in the field by rail and wagon. Timothy O'Sullivan, Andrew Russell, and Brady's cameramen took about one hundred photographs covering operations at the vast City Point facility.

Grant's strategy at Petersburg was not complicated. He planned gradually to extend his lines around the city, forcing Lee to do the same. Eventually Lee, with less manpower and fewer resources, would reach a breaking point.

Both the Union and Confederate forces settled down to a long period of deadly trench warfare. The sides exchanged artillery barrages and mortar fire, while sharpshooters sought to pick off any enemy soldier who showed himself.

Late in June 1864, in a burst of creativity, the commander of a Federal regiment that included many coal miners suggested tunneling under one of the Confederate forts and setting off a monstrous explosive charge. Troops would then pour through the gap in the lines. Grant agreed to give the idea a try. It took about a month to complete the 511-foot tunnel and set the charges. The explosion destroyed the fort, killed or wounded about 276 Confederate soldiers, and sent a great mass of earth into the air. Federal troops rushed into the crater that had been created only to be slaughtered by Confederate troops firing down upon them. Almost 4,000 Union casualties resulted. The Crater, as it came to be called, was a great failure. Grant called it: "The saddest affair I have ever witnessed in the war."

Timothy O'Sullivan, in the employ of Alexander Gardner, Mathew Brady and his assistants, and Andrew Russell were very active during the early weeks of the Petersburg campaign. Brady's crew concentrated on the coverage of artillery batteries and generals and their staffs. Brady himself posed in several photos taken by his cameramen.

Brady and his cameramen withdrew from their frontline positions late in June 1864. O'Sullivan remained active into September and Russell produced a handful of images in December that year. Generally speaking, as the siege wore on, the interest of photographers dwindled.

Wharves and shipping. Alexandria, VA, 1864–1865. Photographer Unidentified

African-Americans unloading ships. City Point, VA, 1864–1865. Photographer unidentified

Waterfront with Federal supply ships. City Point, VA, 1864–1865. Photographer unidentified

Federal supplies at landing. City Point, VA, July 1864.
Photographer unidentified

Artillery at wharf with anchored schooners.
City Point, VA, 1864–1865. Photographer unidentified

B-5283

Coal wharf. City Point, VA,
1864–1865. Photographer
unidentified

Wharves after explosion of
ordnance barges on August 4,
1864. City Point, VA, 1864.
Photographer unidentified

Union army cook. City Point, VA, 1864–1865.
Photographer unidentified

Members of General Grant's staff
(with Mathew Brady at far right). City Pont,
VA, 1864. Photographer unidentified

Locomotive of the U.S. Military Railroad. City Point, VA, 1864–1865. Photographer unidentified

"General J. C. Robinson," military locomotive. City Point, VA, 1864–1865. Photographer unidentified

African American soldier guarding 12-pound Napolean. City Point. VA, 1865. Photographer unidentified

General John A. Rawlins with wife and child at their quarters. City Point, VA, 1864–1865. Photographer unidentified

Federal army wagon wheels. City Point, VA, 1865. Photographer unidentified

Supply wagons of 2nd Brigade, 2nd Corps. City Point, VA, 1865. Photographer unidentified

Railroad bridge across the Appomattox River.
Farmville, VA, vicinity, April 1865.
Timothy O'Sullivan, photographer

Pontoon bridge across the Appomattox River. Broadway Landing, VA, 1864–1865. Photographer unidentified

Ordnance at depot. Broadway Landing, VA, 1865. Photographer unidentified

Ordnance at depot, another view. Broadway Landing, VA, 1865. Photographer unidentified

Tripod artillery swing. Broadway Landing, VA, 1865. Photographer unidentified

Log church built by 50th New York Engineers (with engineer insignia above door). Poplar Grove, VA, June 1864–April 1865. Timothy O'Sullivan, photographer

Company F, 114th Pennsylvania Infantry (Zouaves).
Petersburg, VA, August 1864. Photographer unidentified

Federal fortifications. Petersburg, VA, 1865.
Photographer unidentified

Camp of Oneida, New York, Independent
Cavalry Company. Petersburg, VA, March 1865.
Photographer unidentified

Railroad gun and crew. Petersburg, VA,
1864–1865. Photographer unidentified

Heavy gun mounted at inner line of Confederate
fortifications. Petersburg, VA, April 3, 1865.
Photographer unidentified

The Dictator, 13-inch mortar, in position. Petersburg,
VA, October 1864. David Knox, photographer

Surgeons of
1st Division,
9th Corps.
Petersburg, VA,
October 1864.
Photographer
unidentified

Bombproof shelter in Federal lines. Petersburg, VA, 1864–1865. Photographer unidentified

Officers of 114th Pennsylvania Infantry. Petersburg, VA, August 1864. Photographer unidentified

Company A, Federal Engineer Battalion. Petersburg, VA, August 1864. Photographer unidentified

Sutler's bomb-proof "Fruit and Oyster House".
Petersburg, VA, 1864–1865. Photographer unidentified

Sutler's tent, 2nd Division, 9th Corps. Petersburg, VA,
November 1864. Photographer unidentified

2448

General Grant's headquarters. Petersburg,
VA, 1864–1865. Photographer unidentified

General Orlando Willcox and staff,
3rd Division, 9th Corps. Petersburg, VA, 1864.
Photographer unidentified

Military telegraph operators. Petersburg, VA, August 1864. Photographer unidentified

Military telegraph battery wagon. Petersburg, VA, June 1864. David Knox, photographer

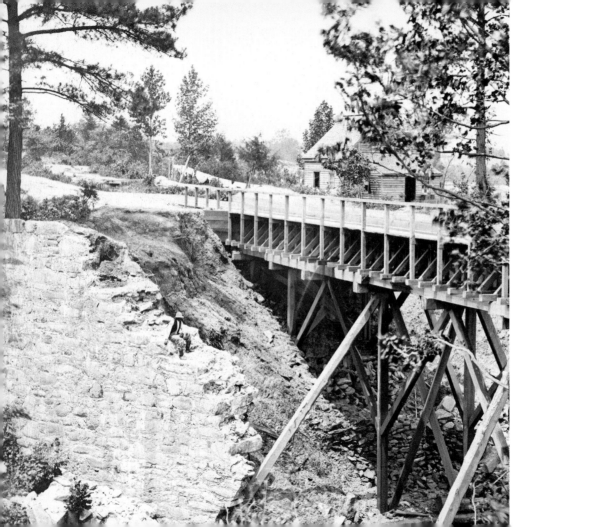

Canal aqueduct. Petersburg, va, vicinity, 1865. Photographer unidentified

Company B, u.s. Engineer Battalion. Petersburg, va, August 1864. Photographer unidentified

Bodies of Confederate and Union dead at
Fort Mahone. Petersburg, VA, April 3, 1865.
Photographer unidentified

Entrance to tunnel beneath Confederate Fort Mahone
(intended to undermine Fort Sedgwick). Petersburg,
VA, April 3, 1865. Photographer unidentified

Body of Confederate soldier. Petersburg, VA, April 3, 1865. Thomas Roche

Body of Confederate soldier. Petersburg, VA, April 3, 1865. Photographer unidentified

Federal soldiers removing artillery from
Confederate fortifications. Petersburg, VA,
April 1865. Photographer unidentified

Pontoon bridges across the Appomattox
River. Petersburg, VA, 1865. Photographer
unidentified

Captured Confederate encampment. Petersburg, VA, June 1864. Photographer unidentified

Summer quarters. Petersburg, VA, August 1864. Photographer unidentified

Interior view, Fort Sedgwick. Petersburg, va,
May 1865. Timothy O'Sullivan, photographer

Bombproof quarters, Fort Sedgwick. Petersburg, va,
1865. Photographer unidentified

Interior view of Confederate
Fort Sedgwick. Petersburg, VA,
May 1865. Photographer
unidentified

Interior view, Fort Stedman. Petersburg, VA, May 1865.
Timothy O'Sullivan, photographer

Confederate fortifications. Petersburg, VA, 1865.
Photographer unidentified

 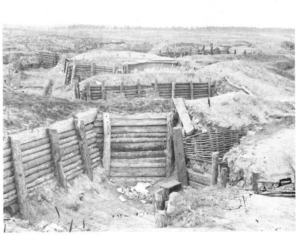

Confederate
fortifications.
Petersburg, VA,
April 3, 1865.
Thomas Roche

Photographers in camp. Petersburg, VA,
1864–1865. Photographer unidentified

Stacked rifles. Petersburg, VA, April 3, 1865.
Photographer unidentified

Soldier's quarters. Petersburg, VA, August 1864. Photographer unidentified

Mills (with photographic wagon of Engineer Department in foreground). Petersburg, VA, 1865. Timothy O'Sullivan, photographer

Federal generals (from left),
Winfield S. Hancock, John
Gibbon, and William Birney.
Petersburg, VA, 1864–1865.
Photographer unidentified

Federal wagon train. Petersburg,
VA, April 10, 1865. John Reekie,
photographer

95

Early in July 1864, General Jubal Early, a six-footer with flashing black eyes and a long grizzled beard, a veteran of First Bull Run, Chancellorsville, Gettysburg, the Wilderness, and Spotsylvania, led 14,000 Confederates across the Potomac River from Virginia into Maryland. Early had been instructed by General Lee to make the move to attract the attention of General Grant. Grant, at the time, had Petersburg, Virginia, under siege. Lee's hope was that Grant would direct troops from Petersburg to counter Early's northward thrust, thus easing pressure on Lee's thin line.

Before long, Early was marching toward Washington. He defeated 7,000 Federal troops under General Lew Wallace at Monocacy, south of Frederick, about forty miles northwest of the capital. Meanwhile, Lee's hope was soon fulfilled, for Grant shifted troops from Petersburg to reinforce Washington. When Early arrived at Washington's northern fringe on July 11 and did some reconnoitering, he saw that the city's fortifications had been strengthened and decided not to attack.

Before Early's withdrawal, the two sides engaged in a firefight at Fort Stevens. It was during this exchange that President Lincoln came under direct Confederate fire. At least twice, Lincoln "exposed his tall form to gaze at bullets from the enemy," according to John Nicolay, Lincoln's private secretary and biographer.

On one of these occasions, Oliver Wendell Holmes, Jr., a Federal captain, not knowing that he was addressing the president, yelled out, "Get down, you damn fool, before you get shot!" Lincoln got down.

Pursued by Federals, Early turned back toward the Shenandoah Valley. But Early's feint on Washington created a furor in the city. It marked the only serious threat that the capital faced during the war.

Washington was fortunate in this regard. By mid-1864, when General Early menaced the city from the north, Washington was entirely capable of warding off an attack. In the early stages of the war, however, conditions were much different; the city was practically defenseless.

The first shots of the Civil War rang out on April 12, 1861, when Confederate forces opened fire on the u.s. garrison at Fort Sumter. By April 14, Sumter was in Confederate hands and Lincoln issued a call for 75,000 troops.

Then, on April 17, the state of Virginia left the Union to join the Confederacy. An armed and hostile foe now lay just across the Potomac River from the nation's capital.

Within hours after Virginia seceded, the state's militia seized Harper's Ferry, the site of a huge Federal arsenal. Before the end of April,

Virginia troops occupied the u.s. naval base near Norfolk.

Maryland, Washington's neighbor to the north and east, a slave-holding border state with strong anti-abolitionist feelings, was another worry. Lincoln worked hard to assure that Maryland remained in the Union. Not long after the clash at Fort Sumter, the 6th Massachusetts Regiment was on the march through Baltimore en route to Washington. Spirited Southern supporters closed in on the troops, shouting and jeering. People began to push and shove. Some threw things. The troops opened fire and bloody fighting followed. Soldiers and civilians were killed. Although the regiment finally got to Washington, the city's rail connection to Baltimore was broken. Not long after, the telegraph wires were cut. Suddenly the nation's capital was isolated.

Lincoln acted quickly. He sent Federal troops to Baltimore to occupy the city. Secessionist members of the Maryland legislature were tossed into jail, as were officials of the city of Baltimore. Such measures were illegal, of course, but they were an indication of how far the president was willing to go to keep Maryland from joining the Confederacy.

Much of Washington was in chaos during this period. Washingtonians seriously wondered whether the city could be protected. Shops were closed and houses boarded up. Emergency plans were made to house the president and his cabinet in the Treasury Building. Sandbag barricades went up at the Treasury's entrance. In the fall of 1861 the Potomac River was closed to ship traffic because the Confederates had set up artillery batteries down river.

The thousands of soldiers who arrived to defend Washington thought of themselves as the city saviors. Washington, however, was inhabited by many with pro-Southern sentiments. They looked upon soldiers from the North with contempt and assailed them with hisses and catcalls when they paraded along Pennsylvania Avenue.

Military leaders realized how vulnerable Washington was to attack and even capture. To put together a plan of defense for the city, General McClellan, commander of the Army of the Potomac, called upon the services of General John Barnard of the Corps of Engineers. The 46-year-old Barnard, though plagued by inherited deafness, had won high praise for his construction of coastal defenses and the navigational improvement of countless rivers and harbors.

For Washington's defense, Barnard directed the construction of 68 enclosed forts and batteries, which were supported by 93 small batteries for field guns. Approximately 400 gun emplacements were also built, and 1,807 cannon and 98 mortars were mounted in them. Twenty miles of rifle pits and thirty miles of military roads ringed the city.

Most of the forts had earthen walls that were supported by logs. Open fields lay in front of the forts. When trees were cut down, their branches were strewn in front of the forts to obstruct enemy infantrymen.

A similar construction campaign turned Washington into a vast hospital complex for treating wounded soldiers. At the outset of the war, the District had only one hospital, staffed by physicians from the medical school and faculty of Columbian College. After the early defeats sustained by the Army of the Potomac, new hospitals were quickly built or public buildings turned into institutions where some degree of medical care could be administered. A wing of the stately Patent Office was turned into the Patent Office Hospital. Reynolds Barracks Hospital was built on what is now the South Lawn of the White House. After the battle of Gettysburg, hospital beds were placed in the marble halls of the Capitol.

By 1865, Washington had sixteen hospitals. Seven others were located nearby in Georgetown, Alexandria, Virginia, and Point Lookout, Maryland.

Washington's many hospitals, with their wounded and sick and medical staffs, the District's extensive system of fortifications, plus the many thousands of troops stationed in the city offered local cameramen an infinite number of subjects to be photographed. These pages represent a portion of their efforts.

Any visitor to Washington today becomes instantly aware of the city's involvement with in Civil War. There's the Lincoln Memorial, of course. There's also the Ulysses S. Grant Memorial at the other end of The Mall. There's the African-American Civil War Memorial and the Nuns of the Battlefield Monument. There are, in fact, forty-one other sculptures in the nation's capital that are directly related to the Civil War.

Washington was never invaded, nor did the capital suffer significant damage during the Civil War. But the city endured a prolonged period of anxiety and hardship, and those days have not been forgotten.

Magazine at Battery Rodgers.
Alexandria, VA, 1861–1865.
Photographer unidentified

Battery Rodgers on the
Potomac River. Alexandria, VA, 1861.
Photographer unidentified

Band of 9th Veteran Reserve Corps. Washington, DC, April 1865. Photographer unidentified

Officers and men of Company K, 3rd Massa-
chusetts Heavy Artillery, at Fort Stevens.
District of Columbia, August 1865.
Photographer unidentified

Detachment of Company K, 3rd Massachusetts
Heavy Artillery, at Fort Stevens.
District of Columbia, August 1865.
William Morris Smith, photographer

Company E, 4th U.S. Colored Infantry, at Fort Lincoln.
District of Columbia, 1861–1865. Photographer
unidentified

15-inch gun and mounting. Washington, DC, vicinity,
1862–1865. Photographer unidentified

Officers of Company F, 2nd New York Artillery, at Fort C.F. Smith. Arlington, VA, August 1865. William Morris Smith, photographer

Company F, 2nd New York Artillery, at Fort C.F. Smith. Arlington, VA, August 1865. William Morris Smith, photographer

Drum Corps
of 10th Veteran
Reserve Corps.
Washington, DC,
June 1865.
Photographer
unidentified

Gate of Fort Slemmer. District of Columbia, 1861–1865. Photographer unidentified

3rd Massachusetts Heavy Artillery at Fort Totten. District of Columbia, August 1865. Photographer unidentified

Officers of Company A and B.
3rd Massachusetts Heavy Artillery,
at Fort Totten. Washington, DC,
1862–1865. William Morris Smith

Chain Bridge over the Potomac
River. Washington, DC, 1865.
Photographer unidentified

Signal Corps quarters near Georgetown. Washington, DC, August 1862. Photographer unidentified

Stored guns at the arsenal. Washington, DC, 1862. Photographer unidentified

Company I, 9th Veteran Reserve Corps, at Washington Circle. Washington, DC, April 1865. Photographer unidentified

Siege gun at Fort Corcoran. Arlington, VA, 1861–1865. Photographer unidentified

Guns and gun crews at Fort Richardson. Arlington, VA, 1861–1865. Photographer unidentified

13th New York Cavalry camp. Prospect Hill, VA, July 1865. Photographer unidentified

Ambulance wagons and drivers at Harewood Hospital. Washington, DC, 1862–1865. Photographer unidentified

Blockhouse near aqueduct bridge. Arlington Heights, VA, 1862–1865. Photographer unidentified

u.s. Sanitary Commission Home Lodge for
Invalid Soldiers. Washington, DC, April 1865.
Photographer unidentified

Disabled soldiers before office of
u.s. Christian Commission. Washington, DC,
April 1865. Photographer unidentified

U.S. Sanitary Commission workers outside
Home Lodge. Washington, DC, June 1863.
Photographer unidentified

Convalescent soldiers outside U.S. Sanitary
Commission Home Lodge. Washington, DC,
April 1865. Photographer unidentified

U.S. Sanitary Commission storehouse and houses. Washington, DC,
April 1865. Photographer
unidentified

Field relief wagons of U.S. Sanitary Commission.
Washington, DC, April 1865. James Gardner,
photographer

Carver Hospital. Washington, DC, vicinity, 1861–1865.
Photographer unidentified

Carver Hospital, interior view. Washington, DC,
vicinity, 1861–1865. Photographer unidentified

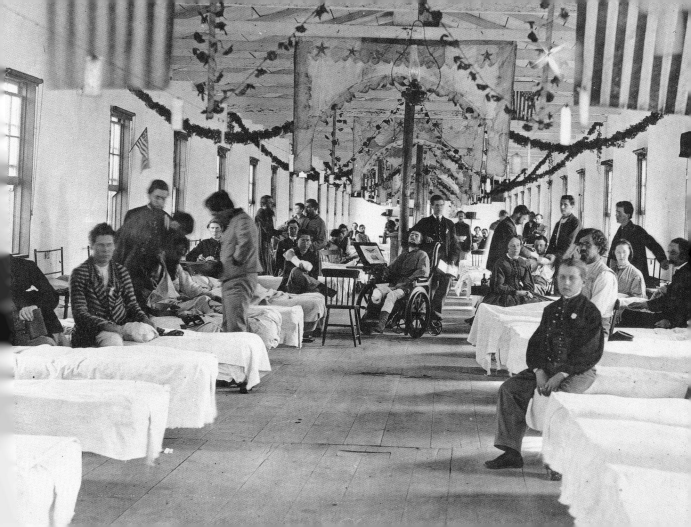

U.S. General Hospital. Washington, DC, vicinity, 1861–1865. Photographer unidentified

Hospital tents behind Douglas Hospital. Washington, DC, May 1864. Photographer unidentified

Ambulance Shop. Washington, DC, April 1865. Photographer unidentified

U.S. General Hospital. Washington, DC, (Potomac Park), 1861–1865. Photographer unidentified

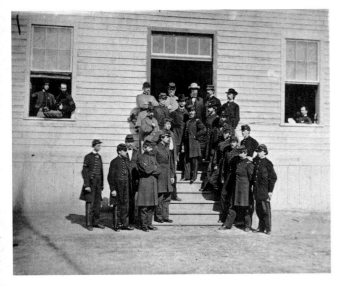

Surgeons and stewards, Harewood Hospital. Washington, DC, 1861–1865. Photographer unidentified

Ward of Harewood Hospital. Washington, DC, 1862–1865. Photographer unidentified

Convalescent camp. Alexandria, VA, 1864. Photographer unidentified

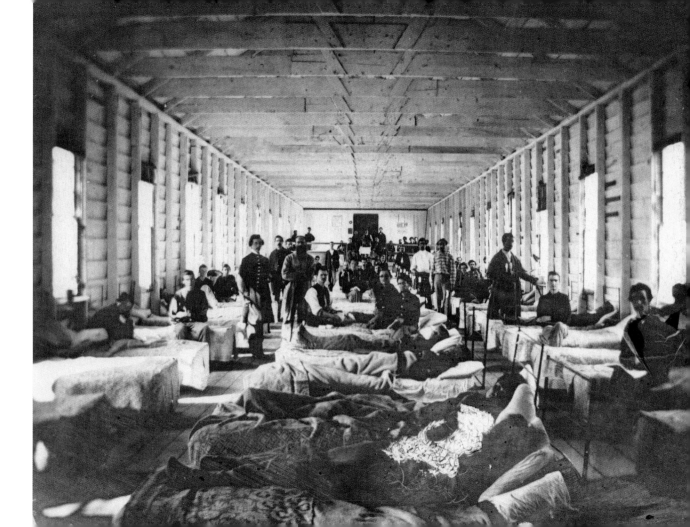

Trimming Shop. Washington, DC, April 1865. Photographer unidentified

Quarters of General Alfred Pleasonton (at right) and Government Horseshoeing Shop. Washington, DC, April 1865. Photographer unidentified

House near Fort Stevens showing effect of damage sustained during General Early's attack. Washington, DC, 1864. Photographer unidentified

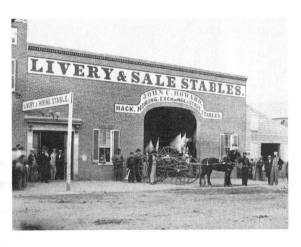

John C. Howard's stable on G. Street between 6th and 7th Streets. Washington, DC, 1865. Photographer unidentified

Government mess house. Washington, DC, April 1865. Photographer unidentified

National cemetery. Washington, DC, 1864–1865. Photographer unidentified

17 Fort Fisher

As the Civil War entered what would be its final year Wilmington, North Carolina, remained the last Confederate seaport on the Atlantic Ocean still open to trade with the outside world. The Lincoln-ordered blockade had shut down all others.

Stout fortifications protected the city from any Union vessels that might make their way up the Cape Fear River. At the river's mouth was Fort Fisher, Wilmington's most formidable bastion.

Although Grant was absorbed with matters at Petersburg, Wilmington and Fort Fisher troubled him. In December 1864, Grant sent a combined army-navy force under General Benjamin Butler and Admiral David D. Porter to subdue the stronghold. The mission failed, at least partly because of Butler's inability to coordinate operations smoothly. Afterward, Butler was relieved of his command.

In January 1865, Grant was ready to try again. In what was the largest army-navy operation of the war, Grant ordered General Alfred Howe Terry, a Yale educated lawyer, to assemble a force of 9,600 men and storm Fort Fisher. Terry was to share leadership of the operation with Admiral Porter, who commanded a flotilla that included sixty gunboats and troop transports.

Shortly after midnight on January 13, Porter's gunboats began their bombardment. The pounding continued for three days. Then Terry's infantrymen landed and started digging in. Some of the war's bloodiest fighting at close quarters took place before Confederate resistance broke.

Once Fort Fisher was in Federal hands, Porter's ships moved up river and began shelling Wilmington. The Confederates evacuated the city on February 22.

Timothy O'Sullivan traveled with Porter's flotilla, presumably on one of the transports, and went ashore shortly after Fort Fisher had been taken. His photographs include general views of the bomb-blasted fortification and its traverses, the earthworks that had been built at right angles to the main work so as to limit the target area offered Federal artillery.

The loss of Fort Fisher was a painful blow to Confederates. As Alexander H. Stephens, Vice President of the Confederacy, was later to admit, "The fall of this Fort was one of the greatest disasters which had befallen our cause from the beginning of the war—not excepting the loss of Vicksburg or Atlanta."

General view, with destroyed gun
carriage. Fort Fisher, N C, January
1865. Timothy O'Sullivan

Interior view, with dismounted
gun. Fort Fisher, N C, January 1865.
Timothy O'Sullivan

348

Interior view, with heavy gun broken
by bombardment. Fort Fisher, NC, January 1865.
Timothy O'Sullivan

Gun with muzzle shot away. Fort Fisher, NC,
January 1865. Timothy O'Sullivan, photographer

Interior view. Fort Fisher, NC, January 1865.
Timothy O'Sullivan

During the early weeks of May 1864, as Grant wrangled with Lee at Spotsylvania, General William T. Sherman led his army out of Chattanooga, Tennessee, on the Georgia border to embark on a series of operations that would bring his Army of the Tennessee into the heart of the Deep South and the gates of Atlanta.

Grant's orders to Sherman were clear. He told the general "to move against General Joseph E. Johnston's army, to break it up, and get into the interior of the enemy's country as far as you can, inflicting all the damage you can against their war resources . . . ."

As Sherman pressed south through northern Georgia during May and June, following the route of the Western and Atlanta Railroad, his army and Johnston's battled or skirmished eight times—in such places as Rocky Face Ridge, Resaca, Rome Crossroads, Adairsville, and Cassville. Late in June, they clashed in heavy fighting at Kennesaw Mountain. In previous weeks, Sherman had been successful in maneuvering Johnston's troops out of position. At Kennesaw Mountain, it was different. Believing that he had a superior force, Sherman ordered an uphill assault against an entrenched enemy. The effort cost Sherman 3,000 casualties, five times as many as Johnston suffered. But Sherman, like Grant, kept pushing ahead, finally forcing Johnston to withdraw to Smyrna and, not long after, to a line along the Chattahoochee River.

Upon reaching the outskirts of Atlanta, Sherman heard the news that Johnston had been replaced by General John B. Hood, who was known for his combative nature. (Hood had lost the use of an arm at Gettysburg and one of his legs at Chickamauga.) Sherman was well aware of Hood's reputation and knew that he could expect an attack. It came on July 20 along Peachtree Creek, north of the city. Both sides suffered heavy losses before Hood was repulsed. Two days later, Hood attacked a second time in what became known as the "Battle of Atlanta." Again the Confederates were turned back, with Hood retreating to the defenses of the city.

Sherman closed in on Atlanta from the north and east first, and then from the south and west. His army was ultimately able to cut off the city's last railroad link to the south. Hood evacuated Atlanta on September 1, 1864. The next day, Sherman sent a telegram to Lincoln that read: "Atlanta is ours, and fairly won." Northerners were exultant over the fall of Atlanta, regarding it as the most important victory of the year.

Sherman paused and rested in Atlanta for more than two months. During that period, George N. Barnard, who had earlier been named the official photographer of Sherman's Army of the Tennessee, and had accompanied the army from Chattanooga to Atlanta, made a documentary record of what Atlanta looked like. Sixty-one of these and other photographs were published in *Barnard's Plates from Photographic Views of Sherman's Campaign* in 1866. (The volume was republished by Dover Books in 1977.) Some of Barnard's images were also used in *Gardner's Photographic Sketch Book of the War*.

Federal pickets before the city.
Atlanta, 1864. George Barnard,
photographer

Federal soldiers at captured fort. Atlanta, 1864. George Barnard, photographer

Chevaux-de-frise on Marietta Street. Atlanta, 1864. George Barnard, photographer

General Sherman and staff at Federal Fort No. 7. Atlanta, 1864. George Barnard, photographer

General Sherman at Federal Fort No. 7. Atlanta, 1864. George Barnard, photographer

Confederate fort. Atlanta, GA, 1864. Photographer unidentified

General Sherman's troops in Confederate fort (east of). Atlanta, GA, 1864. George Barnard, photographer

Ruins of railroad depot, blown up on
Sherman's departure. Atlanta, 1864.
George Barnard, photographer

Wagon train on Marietta Street. Atlanta, 1864.
George Barnard, photographer

365

"Auction & Negro Sales"
building, Whitehall Street.
Atlanta, 1864. George Barnard,
photographer

Whitehall Street, with wagon
train. Atlanta, 1864. George
Barnard, photographer

Shell-damaged Potter house. Atlanta, 1864.
George Barnard, photographer

Federal encampment on Decatur Street. Atlanta, 1864.
George Barnard, photographer

Railroad depot. Atlanta, 1864.
George Barnard, photographer

Railroad yards. Atlanta, GA, 1864.
George Barnard, photographer

2712

19 Sherman's Savannah Campaign

On November 15, 1864, General Sherman began his most famous drive, his 285-mile trek south and east to Savannah and the Atlantic Ocean—his "march to the sea." Before his departure, Sherman sought to render Atlanta useless from a military standpoint, burning a third of the city, including public buildings, foundries, machine shops, and even some residences.

As Sherman's men drove toward Savannah, they encountered little resistance. Traveling without a supply train, Sherman's men foraged for their food, often plundering whatever they came across. Sherman did not order the destruction. But he did nothing to try and stop it.

On December 10, Sherman's army arrived on the outskirts of Savannah. Three days later, his troops captured Fort McAllister, south of the city. On December 22, Sherman sent a telegram to Lincoln that read: "I beg to present you as a Christmas gift the city of Savannah, with 150 heavy guns and plenty of ammunition, also about 25,000 bales of cotton."

Sherman's strategic position was more important to Lincoln than the prizes of war. His army was now poised to surge north and aid Grant in the war's military operation.

Federal soldiers at Fort
McAllister. Savannah, 1864.
Photographer unidentified

Signal station at Fort McAllister.
Savannah, 1864. Photographer
unidentified

Federal soldiers removing ammunition from Fort McAllister. Savannah,
1864. Photographer unidentified

Army engineers removing 8-inch Columbiad gun
from Fort McAllister. Savannah, 1864. Photographer
unidentified

20 Charleston

As General Sherman moved north and into South Carolina, he cut the railroad lines that led to Charleston, isolating the city from the interior and forcing Confederate troops to evacuate the city. On February 18, 1865, Federal troops under the command of General Alexander Schimmelfennig, a Prussian officer, entered the city.

Photographers soon followed. Some recorded the destruction at Fort Sumter that had resulted from attempts to subdue the stronghold during the war. Early in April 1863, a naval force of eight monitors and an ironclad battleship under the command of Admiral Samuel Francis Du Pont attacked Sumter. After five of Du Pont's ships were crippled by heavy fire from shore batteries, the admiral called off the mission.

In September that year, a contingent of Federal marines and sailors attempted a night landing at the fort. When that mission also ended in failure, the Federal Navy gave up hopes of capturing Charleston.

Fort Sumter wasn't the only target for photographers. Some concentrated on Morris Island, in Charleston's harbor, about half a mile from Sumter. In mid-July 1863, Fort (or Battery) Wagner on Morris Island was the scene of a bloody assault by the 54th Massachusetts Regiment of African-American troops. Although the attack was unsuccessful, the valorous action by the regiment helped to increase the acceptance of black troops as part of the Federal army. Not until September 1863, after intense naval bombardment, did the Confederates withdraw from Morris Island.

Once the Federals had installed their Parrot guns on the island, they began raining explosives on Charleston. The bombardment continued for the rest of 1863 and all of 1864. Photographers from both the North and the South recorded the destruction that resulted from these powerful, rifled, muzzle-loading cannons. They were also there to document the Federal flag-raising ceremony at Fort Sumter on April 14, 1865.

Some of the photographs were the work of Samuel Cooley, perhaps the best known of the Civil War photographers to operate below the Mason-Dixon line.

The owner of galleries in Jacksonville, Florida, and Beaufort, South Carolina, Cooley made war scenes not only in Charleston, but also in Savannah, Georgia, and Beaufort and Hilton Head, South Carolina.

City from the roof of the Mills House. Charleston, SC, April 1865. Photographer unidentified

City from the roof of the orphan asylum. Charleston, SC, 1865. Photographer unidentified

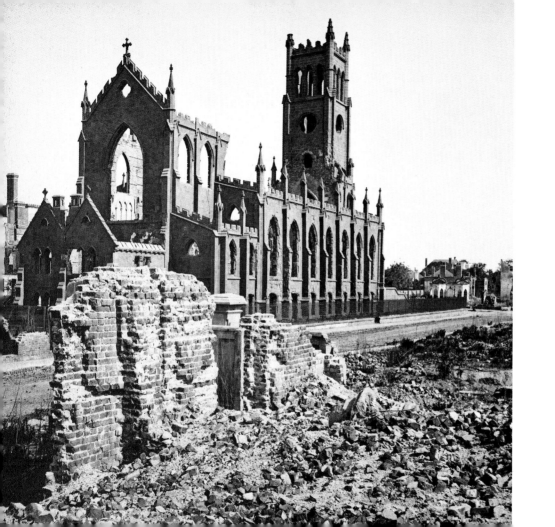

Roman Catholic Cathedral of St. John and St. Finbar. Charleston, SC, 1865. Photographer unidentified

Ruined buildings from the Circular Church. Charleston, SC, April 1865. Photographer unidentified

View of Fort Sumter. Charleston, sc,
April 1865. George Barnard, photographer

O'Connor house in which Union officers
were confined under fire. Charleston, sc,
1865. Photographer unidentified

Site of attack on Fort Sumter, September 8, 1863.
Charleston, SC, 1865. Photographer unidentified

Interior of Fort Sumter. Charleston, SC, 1865.
Photographer unidentified

Beacon on parapet of Fort Sumter.
Charleston, SC, April 1865. Photographer unidentified

Channel side of Fort Sumter.
Charleston, SC, 1865. Photographer unidentified

Fort Moultrie. Charleston, SC, 1865.
Photographer unidentified

North wall of Fort Sumter.
Charleston, SC, 1865. Photographer
unidentified

Fort Johnson, James Island. Charleston, SC, 1865.
Photographer unidentified

Parrott guns inside Fort Putnam, Morris Island.
Charleston, SC, 1865. Photographer unidentified

Flag-raising ceremony at anniversary
of Major Robert Anderson's surrender
(1861). Charleston, SC, April 14, 1865.
Photographer unidentified

Morris Island. Charleston, SC, 1865. Sam A. Cooley, photographer

Ordnance depot, Morris Island. Charleston, SC, 1865. Sam A. Cooley, photographer

Federal mortars aimed at Fort Sumter, Morris Island.
Charleston, sc, 1865. Sam Cooley

Federal squadron at anniversary of Major Robert
Anderson's surrender (1861). Charleston, sc, April 14,
1865. Photographer unidentified

Camera and
wagons of
photographer
Sam A. Cooley.
Unknown
location,
1861–1865.
Photographer
unidentified

21 The Fall of Richmond

In Petersburg during the bitter cold winter of 1864–65, General Lee's troops struggled to survive. Food was in short supply. Sickness and disease were rampant. All the while, Grant kept pressuring his rival, extending his lines westward, forcing Lee to stretch out his beleaguered troops along a front that now covered almost forty miles.

Grant, with his superior force—110,000 men, about twice as many as Lee—was expected to make a move as soon as the warm spring Virginia sunshine dried the mud. But it was Lee who struck first. In the predawn hours of March 25, Lee launched a massive attack upon Fort Stedman, west of Petersburg. In its early stages, the assault was successful. The Confederates captured the fort and occupied three-quarters of a mile of Federal entrenchments.

Then Federal troops counterattacked, pouring troops into the area, pressing the Confederates back to their lines. The assault cost Lee 4,000 casualties.

Grant had already begun the campaign that would bring the war to an end. He had sent General Sheridan's infantry and cavalry to the extreme right flank of Lee's lines. On April 1, Sheridan targeted the road junction of Five Forks, about fifteen miles west of Petersburg. Lee ordered General George Pickett to "hold Five Forks at all hazards." Pickett could not. The Federals broke through the Confederate earthworks, taking more than 4,000 prisoners. Many survivors fled.

Grant now ordered attacks all along the Petersburg line. The Confederates resisted bravely. But Lee, realizing his position was no longer maintainable, ordered that Petersburg and Richmond be evacuated. Federal troops occupied both cities on April 3. Within a week, on April 9, Lee would surrender his Army of Northern Virginia to Grant in a little Virginia town named Appomattox Court House.

Lee's withdrawal from Richmond led to chaos in the city. Before their departure, Confederate troops set fire to the military warehouses along the James River. "The whole river front seemed to be in flames," said General E. Porter Alexander, "amid which occasional heavy explosions were heard . . . ." The flames surged out of control, engulfing the downtown area. Rioters looted warehouses, stores, and even residences.

The fall of Richmond was a wake-up call to photographers. Alexander Gardner is likely to have been the first to respond, arriving at the Confederate capital on April 6. Over the next week or so, Gardner supervised the taking of more than one hundred photographs of the devastated city. About half of these were made by Gardner himself. John Reekie, an employee of Gardner's, accompanied him, and also was active as a photographer.

Mathew Brady traveled to Richmond, too. Brady did not go directly to the city, however. He first visited City Point, just northeast of Petersburg, and there was fortunate enough to be able to photograph General Grant and members of his staff.

In Richmond for several days beginning April 12, Brady's cameramen made about sixty photographs. Brady himself appears in several of these.

Another one hundred or so Richmond photographs were taken by photographers who represented E. & H. T. Anthony Company of New York. Altogether, "no fewer than three hundred photographs were taken in the Confederate capital within two weeks of its fall," says William Frassanito.

General view of burned district.
Richmond, VA, April 1865. Alexander Gardner,
photographer

James River and Kanawha Canal near Haxall Flour Mills. Richmond, VA, 1865. Photographer unidentified

Tredegar Iron Works, with footbridge to Neilson's Island. Richmond, VA, April 1865. Alexander Gardner, photographer

Burned district and the Capitol across the Canal Basin. Richmond, VA, 1865. Photographer unidentified

Destroyed buildings on the banks of the Canal Basin. Richmond, VA, 1865. Photographer unidentified

Destroyed buildings in the burned district.
Richmond, VA, 1865. Photographer unidentified

407

Destroyed buildings in the burned district. Richmond, VA, April 1865. Photographer unidentified

Street in the burned district. Richmond, VA, 1865. Photographer unidentified

View of the city from Gambler's Hill. Richmond, VA, April 1865. Alexander Gardner, photographer

Barges with African Americans on the Canal; destroyed buildings beyond. Richmond, VA, April 1865. Alexander Gardner, photographer

Damaged locomotive, Richmond & Petersburg
Railroad. Richmond, VA, April 1865. Photographer
unidentified

Scattered ammunition near the state arsenal.
Richmond, VA, April 1865. Photographer unidentified

Ruins of paper mill. Richmond, VA, 1865.
Photographer unidentified

Fire engine No. 3. Richmond, VA, 1865.
Photographer unidentified

Custom House and State Capitol. Richmond, VA,
April 1865. Photographer unidentified

Ruins of Richmond & Petersburg
Railroad Bridge. Richmond, VA,
April 1865. Alexander Gardner,
photographer

Ruins of the Exchange Bank. Richmond, VA,
April 1865. Photographer unidentified

417

Ruins of the Southern Express Office. Richmond, VA, 1865. Photographer unidentified

Destroyed railroad cars near Richmond & Petersburg Railroad Station. Richmond, VA, 1865. Photographer unidentified

Residence of General Robert E. Lee.
Richmond, VA, 1865. Photographer
unidentified

Graves of Confederate soldiers in Hollywood
Cemetery. Richmond, VA, 1865. Photographer
unidentified

Grave of General J. E. B Stuart in Hollywood
Cemetery. Richmond, VA, 1865. Photographer
unidentified

View of James
River. Rich-
mond, va, 1865.
Photographer
unidentified

Ruins of state arsenal. Richmond, VA, April 1865.
Photographer unidentified

Park of captured guns. Richmond, VA, 1865. Photographer unidentified

Libby prison. Richmond, VA, April 1865.
Photographer unidentified

Group of African-Americans by canal. Richmond, VA, April 1865. Photographer unidentified

Confederate mountain howitzers. Richmond, VA, April 1865. Photographer unidentified

Damaged locomotives. Richmond, VA, 1865. Photographer unidentified

On May 23 and May 24, 1865, Eastern and Western troops of the Union Army paraded down Pennsylvania Avenue from the Capitol past the White House in what was called a "Grand Review." Author and historian Thomas Fleming, writing in *American Heritage*, called it "the greatest parade in American history."

The nation was still in mourning for the slain Lincoln, victim of the assassin's bullet several weeks before. In Washington, flags flew at half staff, and offices, private homes, and many government and commercial buildings were draped in black. But for the parade the federal government sought to create a festive atmosphere. Teams of workers adorned public buildings with blue-and-white bunting and spanned Pennsylvania Avenue with arches of spring flowers.

In front of the White House, carpenters erected a covered pavilion decorated with flags and flowers for President Andrew Johnson, his cabinet, and high government and military officials. General Grant also occupied the presidential reviewing stand, generously allowing his parading generals to receive the plaudits of the spectators. A second reviewing stand, for members of Congress, Supreme Court justices, and governors of the states, had been erected in Lafayette Park opposite the White House.

Huge crowds flooded into Washington in the days before the event. Every hotel and boardinghouse room was occupied.

At nine o'clock in the morning of May 23, following a loud burst from a signal gun, General George Meade led the Army of the Potomac into Pennsylvania Avenue. The uniforms of the marchers were newly pressed, shoes were shined, and every man shouldered a rifle. Huge bands played "The Battle Hymn of the Republic," "When Johnnie Comes Marching Home," and "Tramp, Tramp, Tramp, the Boys are Marching."

Cheers rang out from the spectators lining the avenue, and many pushed forward to get a closer look. Some called out to men they recognized. "The swaying of their bodies and the swinging of their arms were as measured as the vibrations of a pendulum," Tom Fleming wrote, quoting an eyewitness. "Their muskets shone like a wall of steel."

After General Meade and his staff rode the cavalry and then came regiments of colorful Zouaves. Next, the artillery rolled past, with stern-faced gunners sitting on caissons.

It took seven hours for the Army of the Potomac to complete its march. There was some concern whether the next day's parade, when General Sherman's Army of the Tennessee was set to march, would attract as many spectators. The *New York Times* predicted a "thin crowd."

But the turnout for the Westerners was at least as high as it had been for the Easterners. The *Times* estimated that two hundred thousand spectators were on hand, noting that "thousands left the city after the first day but their places were taken by newcomers."

General William T. Sherman rode at the head of his army. Wreaths of roses circled his horse's head. The *New York World* called the Westerners "hardier, knottier" than their Eastern counterparts. The *New York Tribune* observed their faces seemed "more intelligent, self-reliant, and determined." Some of Sherman's men marched with bare feet. For seven and a half hours, the Army of the Tennessee paraded.

Mathew Brady and his cameramen photographed the Grand Review, setting up their equipment on Pennsylvania Avenue at the point where marchers wheeled right at Fifteenth Street. They produced truly memorable photographs of this notable event.

Cavalry unit approaching presidential reviewing stand. Washington, DC, May 1865. Mathew Brady studio

Artillery unit on Pennsylvania Avenue. Washington, DC, May 1865. Mathew Brady studio

429

Ambulances followed by band and infantry units on Pennsylvania Avenue. Washington, DC, May 1865. Mathew Brady studio

Units of the Army of the Tennessee on Pennsylvania Avenue. Washington, DC, May 1865. Mathew Brady studio

Interior view of Grandstand. Washington, DC, May
1865. Mathew Brady Studio

Spectators at the capitol. Washington, DC, May 1865.
Mathew Brady studio

432

About the Author

George Sullivan has written a good-size shelf of nonfiction books for adults as well as young readers. They reflect a wide range of interests, everything from aviation to archaeology, from baseball to witchcraft. He has written young-adult biographies of Pocahontas and Helen Keller, Abraham Lincoln and George H. W. Bush.

Of Sullivan, Chuck Lawliss, writing in *Publishers Weekly*, said: "Over the years, [he] has mastered the art of writing simply and directly, making complex subjects understandable and interesting . . . ."

Sullivan first became interested in Mathew Brady and his pioneering achievements almost a decade ago when doing research for *Mathew Brady: His Life and Photographs*, a biography for young adults. The book was published in 1994.

According to *The New York Times*, the book is "engrossing." *Kirkus Reviews* called it "illuminating [and] perceptive."

"Sullivan skillfully recounts details of Brady's life and times . . . " said *Booklist*, adding, "Sullivan's text is notable not only for its historical relevance but also for the analogies the author draws between events of Brady's time and events of our own; for example, he refers to the Civil War as the world's first 'living room war' because of Brady's photographs—a characteristic sometimes attributed to the television coverage of the Civil War because of Brady's photographs . . . ."

More recently, Sullivan turned the spotlight away from Mathew Brady toward other Civil War photographers to write *Portraits of War: Civil War Photographers and Their Work*, which was published in 1998. Alexander Gardner, Timothy O'Sullivan, and James Gibson are among the photographers featured in the book.

Reviewers hailed the book for its many dramatic photographs. *Booklist* writes, "Although television brings far more graphic into our homes every day, the grainy pictures these men produced shocked the public in the 1860s and still have the power to startle today."

Sullivan was born in Lowell, Massachusetts, and brought up in Springfield, Massachusetts, where he attended public schools.

He graduated from Fordham University in New York City and worked in public relations there before he began writing on a full-time basis.

Sullivan lives in New York City with his wife. He is a member of PEN, The Authors Guild, and the Society of Writers and Illustrators of Children's Books.

Acquiring Reproductions

In recent years, the Prints and Photographs Division (P&P) of the Library of Congress has digitized thousands of Brady/Civil War images to create a separate and distinct collection within their huge electronic archive. These images are available to anyone with a computer that is linked to the Internet.

To find and download images that appear in this book by means of the Internet, go to the website of the Prints and Photographs Division: *http://www.loc.gov/rr/print/*

Then follow these steps:
- ◆ Click on "P&P Online Catalog"
- ◆ Click on "Search the Catalog"
- ◆ Click on "Searching Numbers"
- ◆ Enter the Digital ID number (LC-dig-cwpb-xxxx or LC-usz62-xxxx) on p. 441f., and click on "Search." (Different versions of each image as well as a variety of file sizes—jpegs and tiffs—can be accessed and downloaded.)

To find additional images not included in this book, a keyword search is recommended. Keywords may include title, subject, format, or associated names.

Quality copies of Brady/CW images can also be ordered from the Library of Congress' Photoduplication Service, whose website is: *www.loc.gov/preserv/pds.*
(Tel. 202 707-5640; Fax: 202 707-1771)

The National Archives has placed the work of making photographic reproductions in the hands of private vendors. These vendors offer a variety of services, formats, and prices. For a listing of vendors, contact the reference staff of the National Archives:

e-mail: stillpix@nara.gov
Tel: 301 837-0561
Fax: 301 837-3621
Mail: Still Picture Reference
Room 5360
National Archives at College Park
8601 Adelphi Rd.
College Park, MD 20740-6001

In the case of a Fax or an e-mail, include your daytime telephone number as well as your postal mailing address.

When seeking to acquire a print, use the "Order No." listed, adding the prefix 111 to that number. For example, the order number for the photograph titled "In the Trenches before Petersburg" is B-768. In executing your order, use 111-B-768.

High resolution digital files of the National Archives images that appear in this book can also be acquired by contacting Athena Angelos at AAngelos@earthlink.net.

While the Still Pictures Branch of the National Archives does not have high resolution images available on its searchable database at this time, you can use this website to view a good portion of their vast holdings:
http://www.archives.gov/research_room/arc/

Order Numbers

from the Library of Congress and National Archives

278   LC-DIG: cwpb 01319
279   LC-DIG: cwpb 01730
280   LC-DIG: cwpb 01991
281   LC-DIG: cwpb 01713
282   LC-DIG: cwpb 00498
283   LC-DIG: cwpb 04330
284   LC-DIG: cwpb 02787
285   LC-DIG: cwpb 04104
286   LC-DIG: cwpb 02550
287   LC-DIG: cwpb 02576
288   LC-DIG: cwpb 02539
289   LC-DIG: cwpb 02555
290   LC-DIG: cwpb 02596
291   LC-DIG: cwpb 01338
292   LC-DIG: cwpb 00382
293   LC-DIG: cwpb 03899
294   LC-DIG: cwpb 04030
294   LC-DIG: cwpb 02582
295   LC-DIG: cwpb 01334
296   LC-DIG: cwpb 02854
296   LC-DIG: cwpb 02785
297   LC-DIG: cwpb 02631
298   LC-DIG: cwpb 00613
299   LC-DIG: cwpb 02647
300   LC-DIG: cwpb 01305
301   LC-DIG: cwpb 03714
302   LC-DIG: cwpb 01701
303   LC-DIG: cwpb 01286

Chapter 16   pp. 304–345
308   LC-DIG: cwpb 01345
309   LC-DIG: cwpb 00636
311   LC-DIG: cwpb 04235
312   LC-DIG: cwpb 04143
313   LC-DIG: cwpb 04043
314   LC-DIG: cwpb 04294
315   LC-DIG: cwpb 04350
316   LC-DIG: cwpb 03989
317   LC-DIG: cwpb 04124
318   LC-DIG: cwpb 04139
319   LC-DIG: cwpb 01506
319   LC-DIG: cwpb 03648
320   LC-DIG: cwpb 04133
321   LC-DIG: cwpb 04113
322   LC-DIG: cwpb 04233
323   LC-DIG: cwpb 04172
323   LC-DIG: cwpb 03649
324   LC-DIG: cwpb 01493
324   LC-DIG: cwpb 01495
325   LC-DIG: cwpb 04178
326   LC-DIG: cwpb 011986
327   LC-DIG: cwpb 01439
328   LC-DIG: cwpb 04160
329   LC-DIG: cwpb 04166
330   LC-DIG: cwpb 04157
331   LC-DIG: cwpb 04155
331   LC-DIG: cwpb 04163
332   LC-DIG: cwpb 04159
332   National Archives: B-380
333   National Archives: B-358
334   National Archives: B-121

335   LC-DIG: cwpb 04322
336   LC-DIG: cwpb 04256
337   National Archives: B-197
338   National Archives: B-2184
338   LC-DIG: cwpb 00486
339   National Archives: B-286
340   LC-DIG: cwpb 04151
341   LC-DIG: cwpb 04318
342   LC-DIG: cwpb 00659
344   LC-DIG: cwpb 04203
344   LC-DIG: cwpb 04306
345   LC-DIG: cwpb 01380

Chapter 17   pp. 346–53
348   LC-DIG: cwpb 03746
349   LC-DIG: cwpb 03918
351   LC-DIG: cwpb 03677
352   LC-DIG: cwpb 00562
353   LC-DIG: cwp 4a39658

Chapter 18   pp. 354–71
357   LC-DIG: cwpb 03388
358   LC-DIG: cwpb 03402
359   LC-DIG: cwp 4a39775
360   LC-DIG: cwpb 03384
361   LC-DIG: cwpb 03379
362   LC-DIG: cwpb 03403
363   LC-DIG: cwpb 03400
364   LC-DIG: cwpb 02226
365   LC-DIG: cwpb 03355
366   LC-DIG: cwpb 03350
367   LC-DIG: cwpb 03466

Photographic Credits

All photographs are the property of
the Library of Congress or the National
Archives, as listed on pp. 440–44, with
the exception of the following:

p. 15: Lloyd Ostendorf Collection
p. 16: National Portrait Gallery,
    Smithsonian Institution
p. 19: New York Public Library,
    New York
p. 24: National Portrait Gallery
p. 28: George Eastman House,
    International Museum of
    Photography, New York
p. 29 top: Sotheby's New York,
    New York
p. 32: private collection

Front cover and p. 1:
Unidentified locations, Brady studio
Spine and frontispiece:
Mathew Brady, c. 1875, Brady studio

The Library of Congress Control
Number: 2004100561
British Library Cataloguing-in-
Publication Data: a catalogue record
for this book is available from the
British Library; Deutsche Bibliothek
holds a record of this publication in
the Deutsche Nationalbibliografie:
http://dnb.ddb.de

© 2004 Prestel Verlag
Munich · Berlin · London · New York

Prestel Verlag
Königinstrasse 9
80539 Munich
Tel. +49 (89) 381709-0
fax +49 (89) 381709-35

Prestel Publishing Ltd.
4 Bloomsbury Place
London WC 1A 2QA
Tel. +44 (020) 7323-5004
fax +44 (020) 7636-8004

Prestel Publishing
900 Broadway, Suite 603
New York, NY 10003
Tel. +1 (212) 995-2720
fax +1 (212) 995-2733

www.prestel.com

Editorial direction:
Christopher Wynne
Design and layout: Matthias Hauer

Typefaces: Monotype Bulmer
and Berthold Akzidenz Grotesk
Origination: Reproline mediateam,
Munich
Printing and binding: Graspo, Zlín

Printed on acid-free paper

ISBN 3-7913-2929-4

Helbling